NOT WORDS

BUT DEEDS

NOT WORDS

BUT DEEDS

Nano Nagle's Daring Venture and the Founding of the Presentation Sisters

CORONA WYSE, PBVM

FLANKER PRESS LTD.
ST. JOHN'S, NL

Library and Archives Canada Cataloguing in Publication

Wyse, Corona, 1917–
    Not words, but deeds : Nano Nagle's daring venture and the founding of the
Presentation Sisters / Corona Wyse.

Includes poetry.
ISBN 1-894463-99-4

    1. Nagle, Nano, 1718–1784. 2. Sisters of the Presentation of the Blessed
Virgin Mary--Newfoundland and Labrador--History. 3. Catholic Church--
Education--Newfoundland and Labrador--History. 4. Sisters of the Presentation
of the Blessed Virgin Mary--Biography. I. Title.

BX4511.Z8W98 2006   271'.97702   C2006-906268-4

PRINTED IN CANADA

FLANKER PRESS
P.O. BOX 2522, STATION C
ST. JOHN'S, NL, CANADA A1C 6K1
TOLL FREE: 1-866-739-4420
WWW.FLANKERPRESS.COM

Cover Design: Adam Freake
freakdesignstudios@nl.rogers.com 709-745-6803

First Canadian edition printed November 2006

10 9 8 7 6 5 4 3 2 1

We acknowledge the financial support of: the Government of Canada through the
Book Publishing Industry Development Program (BPIDP); the Canada Council for
the Arts which last year invested $20.0 million in writing and publishing through-
out Canada; the Government of Newfoundland and Labrador, Department of
Tourism, Culture and Recreation.

DEDICATION

To all our Presentation associates in Newfoundland and Labrador, especially the 2002–2006 group at Gander and Grand Falls–Windsor. To Barbara Barron, John Barron, Madeline Blackmore, Sharon Blandford, Janice Duder, Lucy Dwyer, Marcey Kane, Genevieve Murphy, and Kathleen White, this book is lovingly dedicated. Included here, too, are Marian Gill, Ann Griffin, Madeline Hamilton, Ann Mackey, Carmelita Pittman, and the late Joan Clark—our first associates from Central Newfoundland.

We have been enriched by your experience as associates no less than by your generous spirit of co-operation and sharing. By your prayer, love for the poor, and concern for the marginalized may you all be true friends of Nano Nagle.

This postcard picture of Nano Nagle has her signature copied from a document
signed by her in 1768. Engraving by Charles Turner, 1774–1857.
(Reproduced by courtesy of Presentation
Generalate Monasterevan, Co. Kildare, Ireland.)

CONTENTS

NANO NAGLE, 1718–1784.

Meet a woman whose love was stronger than the viciousness, injustice, greed, and violence that swamped her city and nation.

A woman of indomitable courage, native shrewdness and indefatigable zeal for her faith, unbounded compassion, and radical creativity.

Challenging the brutal power of her people's oppressors, she spent her life on the razor's edge of danger.

(Courtesy of the Presentation Sisters of the Indian Province.)

PREFACE

Convent of the Presentation, Gander, NL
Feast of the Epiphany, 2006

The material in this book was researched and written with much love and care. Because it recounts key events in the life of Nano Nagle, the work gave me great pleasure. This loved Irish lady was the foundress of our religious congregation: Sisters of the Presentation of the Blessed Virgin Mary. This is Part I of the book.

Writing this book with our associates in mind, I decided to include something of the history of the Presentation Sisters in Newfoundland. Sister Mary James Dinn, PBVM, of loved memory, had written a rather comprehensive little book on this very topic in 1975 as part of our bicentennial celebrations. I have transferred here a major portion of the section in her book entitled *Bishop Fleming Brings Presentation Sisters to Newfoundland* (15-20 and parts of 25-6). This forms Part II of this book.

Part III contains poems eulogizing Nano Nagle and written chiefly by Newfoundland Presentations, plus two lovely ones by the late Sister Raphael Consedine, PBVM from Australia.

Some pertinent and interesting articles from our archives constitute Part IV.

It is my hope that this small contribution to the quite formidable array of books on Nano Nagle will inspire emulation of her spirit. Hopefully, too, the reader will gain a deeper insight into the contribution made to education in Newfoundland by the Presentation Sisters.

For further information on Nano Nagle and the Presentation Sisters of Newfoundland and Labrador, please visit www.presentationsisters.ca.

I

Nano Nagle and Ireland 300 Years Ago.
The Founding of the Sisters
of the Presentation of the
Blessed Virgin Mary

Introduction

About the middle of the eighteenth century a new apostle came to the Irish scene. A new St. Patrick arose to rekindle the faith of the Irish people who for two hundred years had been ground into the dust by Ireland's infamous penal laws. This valiant woman, a torchbearer in one of the darkest periods of Ireland's history, was none other than Nano Nagle, saintly foundress of the Presentation Sisters.

Early Life

*B*orn in Ballygriffin, County Cork, Ireland, in 1718, of a wealthy middle-class family, Honora "Nano" Nagle like most girls of her station, was sent to France to receive the education denied to Catholics in Ireland. Even this was forbidden by the penal laws, so she was smuggled to France.

Education completed, she was introduced to the fashionable circles of Paris and spent her days in a round of festivities—a life she thoroughly enjoyed. Grace struck unexpectedly and forcibly one early morning when, on returning from a ball, she noticed on the steps of a church a group of people, lunch pails in hand, waiting to assist at Mass before beginning their work in the fields. She compared her value system with theirs and the reflection moved her deeply. That was her last ball. In 1746, her father died and she and her sister, Ann, returned to Dublin where her mother was then living.

Here I Am,
Lord,
Send Me!

It was here, in Dublin, that Nano received her call to help the poor. Looking for a piece of Parisian silk one day to make a new gown for herself, she learned from Ann that the latter had sold it and given the money to the poor.

Nano was so deeply touched that she herself asserted years later that it was this incident that decided her vocation. Ann's death shortly afterwards reinforced Nano's decision to do all she could for the poor. On a visit to her brother in Ballygriffin, her ancestral home, Nano's resolve deepened. Moving among servants and tenants, she realized the depth of their ignorance of religion and the errors and superstitions with which they were imbued. As Rev. Dr. Coppinger, a contemporary of hers, says in his *Life of Nano Nagle* written in 1794:

> Under a misconception of their obligations, they substituted error in the place of truth; while they kept up an attachment to certain exterior observances, they were totally devoid of the spirit of Religion; their fervour was superstitious, their faith was erroneous, and they had no charity. Licentiousness, while it could bless itself, and tell its beads, could live without remorse, and die without repentance; sacraments and sacrilege went hand in hand, and conscience was at rest upon its own strings. . . .[1]

Seeing no way in which she could possibly alleviate this excess of misery, Nano decided to consecrate her life to God and spend her days in prayer for the poor of Ireland in a cloister in France. However, God had other plans for her. Constantly haunted by her knowledge of the ignorance and misery of the poor in Ireland whom she felt were calling her back to help them, Nano confided her desires and worries to her Jesuit Confessor. Recognizing the workings of grace, he advised her to return to Ireland. All her remonstrations and arguments that there was nothing she could do about the situation were in vain. Her confessor was adamant: God was clearly calling her back to teach the Irish children.

Apostolate to the Poor

Invited by her brother and sister-in-law to make her home with them, Nano returned to Cork, her mind made up to begin a little school. Biding her time, she finally rented a small, two-room mud cabin. Prudently, she remained in the background and conducted her business through her maid who gathered thirty little girls. Her dream was realized. The school had started. This was 1754 or 1755, maybe even as early as 1749–50.

> Fearing her brother's anger, she said nothing to him about the project for he was in a position where reprisals could be taken. When he did find out quite by accident some months later, he was indeed quite angry but finally came around to seeing her point of view. So many were the children who wanted to be admitted to her school that she procured another cabin close by and within nine months she had two hundred children packed in the two cabin schools. Soon, well-to-do Catholics in the northern part of the city begged for a school, promising financial aid — which promise was short-lived. However, it was not long before she had two hundred more children in a two-storey house in the northern part of the city. Thus far her one concern was girls. However, her sister-in-law pushed for a school for boys, making the

family's financial aid dependent on its realization. Submitting to her family's wishes, she obtained another cabin near the first two (in Cove Lane) and she hired a Master to teach the forty boys who came. Her meagre resources had reached the draining point but she was determined nothing would happen to her schools. Things eased financially in 1757 when her Uncle Joseph died, leaving her a considerable fortune.

Thus, within a period of two years, Nano had four schools and 440 pupils. In a letter of July 17, 1769, she could write that she had five schools for girls and two for boys. The latter, she tells us in the same letter, learned to read, and when they had the Douai Catechism by heart they learned to write and do Arithmetic. For the girls, instead of Arithmetic, Needlework and Spinning were substituted. Nor did Nano merely stress rote memory in the study of the Catechism. She tells us in the same letter that she explained the Catechism in one school or another every day. In addition, she prepared a group for first Confession in each of her seven schools twice a year, and another group for First Holy Communion. She made little of a health problem which developed at this time and soon wrote that she was feeling no ill effects of her lung weakness. "If anyone thought as little of labour as I do, they would have little merit," she writes. "I often think my schools will never bring me to heaven as I only take delight and pleasure in them."[2]

> 'When the work of
> school was over
> she turned her
> steps to the
> lanes and alleys
> to bring comfort
> to the poor,
> the aged and
> infirm.
> It was said of
> her that there
> was not a
> garret in Cork
> that she had
> not visited.
> 'She built on
> LOVE.'
> T. J. Walsh

Nano Nagle

Nor did Nano's work cease with the end of a school day. Working girls came for Rosary and instruction for an hour each evening. Furthermore, the poor and the lonely, the sick and the dying received her ministrations at night as, with a lantern to guide her, she traversed the Cork alleys where disease was rampant and hygiene unknown—alleys that were no wider than the span of one's arms. As Walsh in his biography points out, "Fevers and infection had no terrors for the servant of Christ. Her privilege was to watch over the pallets of the dying." The annalist at South Presentation Convent records that there was not a garret in Cork that Nano did not know and visit.[3]

As Sister Miriam Martin, PBVM, says in one of her spiritual/musical compositions, "Fire to the Rock":

> *In the story of Earth Life a new time unfolds*
> *The footsteps on Nano her lantern light bold,*
> *To shine on the faces of those*
> *Held in the dark.*

Ireland in the Eighteenth Century

Let us take a look at the Ireland of Nano Nagle's day in order to better understand the milieu in which she worked and the forces with which she had to contend.

> By the end of the 17th century the old Gaelic state was totally suppressed, the Protestant ascendancy enjoyed a complete monopoly of all political power and social privileges. . . . The defeated Irish culture

was to be uprooted and destroyed. . . . To achieve this, a series of laws was enacted, known in history as the penal code. The scheme was not one of persecution; rather it was an attempt to demoralize a whole nation. It was sought at any cost to keep the Catholics in ignorance, misery and slavery, and it was this mentality, which governed all attempted social reforms, even in the late 18th century.[4]

Not only were Catholics excluded by law from all public life and, indeed, a great deal of normal social activity, but it was considered absolutely essential that the direction and control of education be taken out of their hands. Justifying the penal laws, John Locke, the political theorist, who greatly influenced educational philosophy, stressed that no man was born a papist but rather that popery was acquired through education and environment. Arguing that a Protestant environment would create a loyal Protestant nation, he advocated that only the very rudiments of education should be allowed to Catholics and, furthermore, they should be kept in a position that in no way fitted them for public office or political freedom. Swift, Berkeley and a host of other influential writers and intellectuals of the day subscribed to this viewpoint. In fact, at one time it was even declared by both the Lord Chancellor and the Chief Justice that the law didn't exist for the benefit of an Irish Catholic, nor even presume an Irish Catholic to exist. Thus cut off from the rest of society, and from normal legal process, the vast majority of the Irish people were isolated as an inferior race. It is true that some Catholics did succeed in holding their position among the gentry, either by skilful circumventing of the law, through the co-operation of good Protestant friends, mere luck, or by changing interests from land to commerce.

As the Protestant ascendancy sought to grab up land, there were wide-scale evictions—as there also were if taxes couldn't be paid. The peasants were thus forced to the hilly regions, where the most meagre existence was eked out on potato patches—the source of their total existence. When the potato crop failed, as it did notably in 1728–29 and again in 1740–41, a great famine resulted in the death of 300,000 people. Whole villages were wiped out through hunger and disease. Berkeley stated that in one parish alone five hundred people died daily. Another letter of the time stated that "multitudes perished in ditches and under hedges. Old men were seen eating grass like beasts. Helpless orphans died in dunghills with none to take them in for fear of infection."[5]

Writing in 1720, Dean Swift, the Irish clergyman satirist, could say that the Irish tenant of his day was worse off than the English beggars. A few years later the Protestant bishop of Derry wrote of a journey through Ireland: "Never did I behold in Picardy, Westphalia or Scotland, such dismal marks of hunger and want as appeared on the countenances of the poor creatures I met on the roads of Ireland." The philosopher-Bishop Berkeley wondered "whether there be on earth any Christian or civilized people so beggarly, wretched and destitute as the common Irish." Again he says,

> The houses of the poor are scenes of poverty; within you see a pot and a little straw; without, a heap of children tumbling on a dunghill. In every road the ragged ensigns of poverty are displayed. You often meet caravans of poor—whole families in a drove, without any clothes to cover them or bread to feed them.[6]

Even with the improvement of the lot of the upper and

middle classes as the eighteenth century progressed, the situation of the poor remained the same.

> The social and economic stress of the time was increased by a spectacular increase in population after the middle of the 18th century—just when Nano Nagle was beginning her schools. This resulted from early marriages where the average age was 18 or 19 for boys and 16 or 17 for girls. With nothing to look forward to, there was little point in waiting. The standard of living was so low that all that was needed was a scrap of land, a mud hut erected in a couple of days, a cooking utensil and maybe a stool. Daily marriages were contracted with reckless lack of foresight. As the population increased, land became pure gold. Children settled on their parents' land, the only alternative to starvation. In turn, they allowed their children the same privilege. The result was that in a comparatively short time, four, five or even ten families were living on a piece of land that could not adequately support one family.[7]

At this time the solicitor general for Ireland stated that "the majority of tenants were worse off than the beasts in their fields."[8] The wages of an agricultural worker were eight pence for a twelve-hour day, five pence for a woman. It is no wonder that a commissioner from Cashel could write that he had visited the huts of the poor and found that there were 500 families without a blanket to cover them—and this out of a population, in Cashel, of slightly over 1,300 families at the time. Indeed, "In the 18th century it was not an uncommon thing that a family would have sufficient clothing to allow but one member to attend Sunday Mass."[9]

Conditions of poverty were not confined to rural areas. Dublin, with a population of 172,000 at this time (mid-eighteenth century), did, indeed, have a section of imposing buildings where the aristocracy and the well-to-do middle class lived. But the poor lived in utter destitution in most cases, crowded in lanes, alleys, and courts that were dark, filthy, and disease-ridden. Similar situations existed in all other Irish towns—Cork, Galway, Limerick, Kilkenny, Waterford. As one eyewitness of the time noted: "Our wonder was not that people died but that they lived." He added, "The lives of many have been prolonged, perhaps saved, by that long apprenticeship to want in which the Irish peasant has been trained, and by that lovely touching charity which prompts him to share his scanty meal with his starving brother."[10]

The people still clung to the faith; it was their sole consolation. However, the lack of priests, churches, and schools—all of which were forbidden by the penal laws—left much to be desired in the moral attitudes of the poor. Speaking of what Nano Nagle was brought face to face with at this time, Rev. Dr. Coppinger states: "But how was she afflicted to perceive that these poor creatures were almost absolute strangers to everything she questioned them about."[11] And what of the children whom she sought out to bring to her schools? They roamed the streets, undisciplined, wild, rough, often delinquent and strangers to the refining influences of religious training.

As for education, all that was open to the poor of the time were the charity schools and the charter schools—both of which were condemned by the English philanthropist, John Howard, as being "dens of cruelty and exploitation of child labour."[12] There were also privately organized schools whose sole object was proselytism. The hedge schools were only for those who could pay.

There must have been other Catholics of

THE HEDGE SCHOOL

Illustrated by Eileen Coghlan.
(Source: *Nano Nagle, Lover of Children: Friend of the Poor,*
Sister Immaculata Carr North Presentation Convent, Cork.

the Nagle standing. There were. There was a group of
Catholic gentry who, as noted before, had managed to keep
their lands and/or their wealth. However, though they did
do much for the Catholic political life of the nation, their
chief concerns and main interests centred around the middle
class. One example of this is seen in the type of schools that
arose as soon as the penal laws were repealed in 1782. A

multitude of classical and mathematical schools sprang up to take care of the education of the wealthy because trouble in France at this time prevented their being educated in that country. The poor were given little thought. In fact, as in England and on the continent at the time, the thinking was to keep the poor in their lowly place, else who would do the brawny work—they were the "hewers of wood and drawers of water." The only link between the middle and the lower classes of Irish Catholics was their religion. In language (the middle class spoke English, the peasants, Gaelic), in political concepts, in social and cultural values, the middle class were English-oriented. The large, poorer, helpless, and inarticulate class of Catholics had their own living, ancient culture. They were,

> . . . crushed into the dust by oppressive laws, dying by the thousands of periodic famine and disease, sunk in poverty and misery, and sporadically continuing in illegal organizations in self-defence against the ruthless tyranny and avarice of the Ascendancy.[13]

Nano, Apostle of the Poor

It was onto this scene of moral abuse, social disorder, poverty, ignorance, and the machinations of proselytism that Nano Nagle came in the mid-1700s. It was in this setting that she planted the seed that was to alleviate the

spiritual, intellectual, and even physical misery of the Irish poor—a seed that was to grow into a mighty oak that would spread to every continent and many countries.

Within a few years Nano had seven schools—five for girls and two for boys—where she taught and catechized for four or five hours daily. As sole supervisor of these schools, she carried out her work with undaunted courage despite the great physical strain which the teachings and journeys to and from the schools entailed.

Nano was working in three parishes in Cork. In Cove Lane, Parish of St. Finbar, she had two schools for girls and one for boys, and the same in Cathedral Parish. At Cross St. she also had a school. "Her journey was at least two miles as the crow flies, not to mention rough paths and hills."[14] But Nano was not daunted by difficulty. She carried out this routine for thirty years—some writers say forty.

Rev. Dr. Coppinger tells us in his biography that she "often declared" to being "absolutely terrified" at the "wicked-ness" of her young students. "From this," he says, "we are warranted to suppose that the vulgar world in miniature was delineated in this little assembly" . . . all this in addition to the infected air she had to breathe in a stuffy room, the nauseating smell of their rags and also their nasty ways. All of which only proved "how much they needed all her attention, and that without patience, prayer, and perseverance she could never hope to make a lasting impression."[15]

As the years went by, Nano thought more and more of giving permanency to her work. She wanted nothing to happen to her schools. By 1767, she resolved to introduce a religious order into Ireland to carry on her work with and for the poor. Accordingly, after much effort and many trials, several Irish girls, who had offered to be trained by the French Ursulines, began an

Ursuline foundation in Cork—the whole effort being financed by Nano. Bitter disappointment met her in this project. When the nuns opened their schools in 1772, she found that because of their rule of enclosure they could not go out to her schools—and only one of her schools fell within their enclosure. Nano had hoped that in view of conditions in Ireland the Ursulines there would discontinue their rule of enclosure. It was not to be. Moreover, only a portion of their work could be done with the poor because Ursulines are also called to an Apostolate to the more affluent society, though "they taught all—the children of the wealthy and of the poor without distinction. Theirs was a wide and generous charity to female youth in all lands."[16] All this setback after five years of praying, correspondence, working, planning, building, and the expenditure of much money! Despite this, however, her love and solicitude for the Ursulines never wavered and, ever concerned for their well-being, she continued to contribute to their financial support.

Nano was a woman who dared to let herself be guided by the Spirit of God

Realizing that "her schools could offer only a brief respite from ignorance unless some method was devised to give them permanence" and that "the hovels and garrets of Cork would always have their tenants whose only support was God's grace," Nano formed her plans. "She had neither canonical precedent nor authoritative guidance to direct her steps to the purpose she had in mind."[17]

The Founding of the Congregation

In January 1775, at Nano's invitation, two Cork girls, Elizabeth Burke and Mary Fouhy, joined her in the Apostolate of Charity, which was concentrated solely on the poor. The three took up their abode in Nano's little cottage. As Walsh points out, "The decision was not an act of impulse; rather it was the logical development of a purifying struggle of over twenty years. In the unfolding of time Nano found herself in the role of a religious foundress."[18] She felt she was being called to found a new congregation whose members, as we read in the annals of the South Presentation Convent, Cork, "devoted themselves solely to works of charity among the poor; and seeking them out in their hovels of misery, want and woe."[19] Joined by a fourth young lady, Ann Collins, on Christmas Eve, 1775, Nano was ready to have a vision become a reality, and religious life was begun. The following June 24, 1776, the four received the religious habit. Nano chose the name Sister John of God, Elizabeth Burke became known as Sister Augustine, Mary Fouhy as Sister Joseph, and Ann Collins as Sister Angela. The seed of a new religious congregation was sown. To it Nano gave the name "Sisters of the Sacred Heart of Jesus" (Later, after Nano's death, with enclosure and papal approval, the congregation was called Sisters of the Presentation of the Blessed Virgin Mary.) Nano and those first Sisters made Religious Profession on June 24, 1777. On the same day, Dr. Butler, Bishop of Cork, who presided at the Profession, also officially confirmed Nano's status as Superior of the new Institute.

The twenty or more years that immediately preceded this great step taken by Nano were a beautiful and solid preparation for the consecration of her life to God in this formal way. Two complimentary pen-pictures of these years, written by Dr. Coppinger, capture beautifully Nano Nagle, the contemplative-in-action:

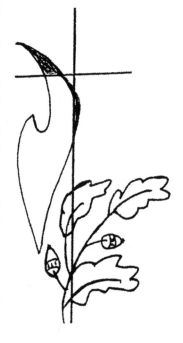

At the Chapel every day during the Divine service. . . . silent, motionless, absorbed in recollection . . . How often have we seen her, after a well-spent day, returning through the darkness of the night, dripping with rain, mingled in the bustling crowds, moving thoughtfully along by the faint glimmering of a wretched lantern, withholding from herself in this manner the necessaries of life to administer the comfort of it to others . . . Then after her plain frugal reflection she would retire to her evening devotions, which she performed in her apartment where, in converse with the Great Teacher of truth, she advanced in the Science of the Saints, and renewed her fervour for the day ensuing.[20]

In addition, we are told that she fasted every Wednesday and Friday on bread and water and took the discipline four times a week. Her sisters in religion have told us that she spent four hours, five o'clock to nine, each morning on her knees in prayer. [21] Such an ascetical life, combined with the hardships of her strenuous active apostolate, must indeed have drawn down an abundance of God's blessings on her loved poor. Nano's duties as superior of the new religious institute did not in any way detract from her work among the poor children. Nor did she stop at schools for the poor. In 1779, listing the works of a French Order, she wrote:

> In some houses they take care of the sick; there are others where they instruct the orphans, others where they take care of old men and women . . . They have penitents . . . and in some places they are of great service to prisoners. We are obliged to most of these charities, only we must prefer the schools to all the others.[22]

Her schools took precedence, but there were focal points of numerous acts of charity. Dr. Coppinger refers to "disconsolate widows, forlorn orphans, reduced housekeepers, and superannuated tradesmen"[23] whose wants she took care of so often. In 1783, a year before her death, she writes that she was building an almshouse for old women. (The Sisters took care of this charitable work for over one hundred years, until the Little Sisters of the Poor came to Ireland.) Her final dream, unrealized because she was claimed by death, was to build a home for penitent women.

If the branch remains firmly attached to the vine,

it bears much fruit.

John 15:5

Nano, the Valiant Woman

We can have some idea of the courage and moral stamina of Nano Nagle when we consider that this quiet little lady, frail of health and small of stature, faced the unknown and dared to open schools when the penal laws positively forbade such action. King William's Law was still on the books. It ran thus:

> . . . No person whatever of the popish religion shall publicly or in private house, teach school, or instruct youth in learning within this realm upon pain of £20, and of being committed to prison for the space of three months for every offence.[24]

Despite the poverty rampant at the time, no one ever informed on her schools. At this time £50 was offered for the apprehension of a Catholic priest, £150 for a bishop, and £500 for the conviction of anyone sheltering a priest. Moreover, a ruling of Queen Elizabeth stated that any religious ordained or professed was guilty of high treason. This was still on the Statute Book when Nano Nagle brought the Ursulines to Ireland and when, a few years later, she herself was professed. Furthermore, religious community life as such had ceased to exist in Ireland in the latter part of the seventeenth century—1698 to be exact—though two cloistered Orders, the Dominican Sisters and the Poor Clares, found safe havens that enabled them to live in secret. Nano's determination and unflinching courage are astounding. It is worth noting that in a book, *Lettres Spiritualles,* which Nano used for spiritual reading and which is preserved in South Presentation Convent, Cork, a number of passages are marked in pencil by her. One of these, translated, reads ". . . Work well and wait for nobody; don't be afraid to go it alone. . . . It is the grace of God that inspires you."[25] The words seem to have been a guiding light to her, so well do they epitomize her daring spirit.

Nano Nagle's determined persistence in carrying out her proposed plans and allowing nothing to stand in her way is exemplified in a number of instances. For example, as mentioned above, when beginning her schools she kept all her plans to herself. The first school was in operation for three months before her brother, with whom she made her home, learned about it quite accidentally. The same quiet determination and prudence surrounded her plans to bring the Ursulines to Ireland. Not even with her immediate family did she discuss it. Again, when the Ursuline foundation was in progress, Bishop Butler of Cork said he would be better pleased if she had the Protestant consent for the establishment. Her reply to the gentleman who brought the request is expressed in a letter she wrote on July 20, 1770: "I told him before my brother and sister that had I consulted my own family, I should not have had a school in Cork."[26] In a similar way, toward the end of her life, when the penal laws were on the way out, Catholic schools were allowed provided one took the oath of allegiance and received a licence from the Protestant Bishop of the place. On the surface, it looks as if Catholic schools were being tolerated. In reality, however, the purpose of the ruling was to control those schools which, in defiance of the law, had been set up. Nano did not ask that approval. (She had already been teaching twenty-five years. After 1792, no such licence was required, but its procurement meant exemption from window tax).

The Ursuline Sisters, who held her in the greatest esteem, were constantly begging her to come and live in the convent she had built for them. She consistently refused. While she did not eat with them either, she did accept the meals they sent her, often recreated with them, and each Saturday evening instructed their boarders. On one occasion, while she was out, they took her bed and brought it to the Ursuline convent. "The attempts were fruitless; on her return Nano caused the alterations to be undone with a finality that taught them that their hopes would never be realized."[27]

Nano's quiet determination was nowhere more evident than in the building of her convent, which was begun in 1775. The site chosen was quite close to the Ursuline convent. These sisters did not welcome the fact that Nano's solicitude was being diverted from themselves. In addition, they feared the resentment of the Protestant Ascendancy with a second religious house in such close proximity. Dr. Moylan, Parish Priest of St. Finbar's and later Bishop of Kerry, agreed with them and spoke to Nano about it. She listened respectfully and quietly to his appeals but remained firm in her decision. Then he appeared at the building site and threatened to destroy what was erected of the building if she did not build at the other end of the city. The Presentation annalist tells us:

> She mildly bowed beneath the pressure of his displeasure only saying that if he was pleased to drive her thence she would never pursue her intended object in Cork, but would retire to some other part of Ireland where she would meet with no opposition and more encouragement to effect her purposes on behalf of those whom she always carried in her heart — the poor.[28]

Father Moylan, not willing to lose her from Cork, permitted her to continue her project. He later "became her most enthusiastic ally in all her plans."[29] In fact, the new convent did not arouse any resentment in the Protestant Ascendancy. Nano, however, was careful, again, to do things in her own quiet and unobtrusive way. When the sisters finally took up their abode in the new building in 1780, she exercised all caution in moving in. She writes in a letter dated July 29, 1780:

> When the disturbances broke out in London, I was afraid to venture, imagining the same contagious frenzy may break out in this Kingdom. So I waited until the time seemed quite peaceful, yet notwithstanding we stole like thieves. I got up before three in the morning and had all our beds taken down and sent to the house, before anyone was up in the street. I begged the Ladies not to say a word about it to any of their company that came to see them. Nor did I let any person know in the town of my friends, as I was sure that by acting in this manner the good work could be carried on much better than in making any noise about it. We moved on the 15th of July, so we were there for the festival of our Blessed lady, under whose protection we are . . .[30]

The first Presentation Convent in Cork to house Nano's own community, 1775. Taken from *Flame of Love*, by Sister Rosaria O'Callaghan, PBVM, 1960. (Courtesy of the Presentation Sisters Aberdeen, South Dakota, USA.)

The convent Nano built for the Ursuline Sisters whom she invited from France, 1771.
Taken from *Flame of Love*, by Sister Rosaria O'Callaghan, PBVM, 1960.
(Courtesy of the Presentation Sisters, Aberdeen, South Dakota, USA.)

Mother Nagle's original eighteenth-century school with the top floor added. Taken from *Flame of Love*, by Sister Rosaria O'Callaghan, PBVM, 1960. (Courtesy of the Presentation Sisters, Aberdeen, South Dakota, USA.)

The building of this first convent was actually completed in 1777, but due to a part of the wall in their yard being broken down during construction of the garden, the back part of the house was exposed and so, for another reason, she says, "It was not safe to venture."[31] They did hold classes in the new house and, typical of Nano, it was given a special symbolic blessing on Christmas Day, 1777, when she invited fifty beggars to dinner and she and the other sisters waited on them. (This custom was kept up at South Presentation Convent for 110 years.)

With an ever-watchful eye she guarded her beloved schools, wanting and expecting always the best in care and instruction. Without second thought she dismissed those teachers who did not measure up to her standards. She writes in 1778, three years after founding her own religious institute:

I discharged the mistresses, all except one whom I had employed such a number of years that I could not part with her. As to the others, I had great fault to find with them that live at a great distance from me; and I could not see the schools taken care of, only on certain days in the week. I should, I am afraid, never have had courage to undertake this establishment, only seeing how improper seculars, that did it only for bread, were to take care of poor children; it must be them that have true zeal. We have the charge of them ourselves and thank God they never were tended as at present in every respect.[32]

Everything in her power was done by this great woman of purpose to ensure that the work she had begun would continue and prosper. Soon, however, money became a problem. Having purchased the seven cabins for schools, paid all the teachers, built and endowed the Ursuline convent, and paid all expenses connected with the training of Ursuline novices destined for Ireland, and finally, built her own convent, Nano realized that her fortune had rapidly been depleted. Soon she found herself in financial difficulties. She writes in 1778: "The building I undertook at a time I could not afford it, has much perplexed me to get money to go on with it."[33] Little money came from the Catholics in the north end of the city, who had originally promised to finance the school in that area, for which they had begged. The Nagle family couldn't supply all that was needed. A group of Catholics who had promised to gather funds fell down on the job. What did Nano do? She begged for her beloved poor—practically from door to door.

Indeed, begging for alms continued to be a part of her charitable works up to the last weeks of her life. She often met with rebuffs and insult, but she bore it patiently, even with joy. One incident is preserved in the Presentation Annals:

> Nano entered the shop of a merchant who regularly contributed to her schools. A rough-spoken assistant, failing to recognize Miss Nagle, ordered her to leave. Nano replied that she would await the return of his employer. Several times the assistant requested her in rude terms to depart, but to no avail. When the merchant returned a complaint was made that an importunate old mendicant was in his shop for two hours awaiting his appearance. The merchant was amazed to see that the despised beggar woman seated on a pile of skins at the door of his shop was Miss Nagle, the woman, says the annalist, whom of all others upon earth he venerated most. Covered with shame and confusion he loaded her with apologies and kindness.[34]

It was not only on behalf of her schools that she begged. Coppinger notes "that she, like the man in the Gospel, had considered a field and bought it. The field was eighteenth-century Cork with its forlorn orphans, disconsolate widows, its fetor, its press gangs, its faction fights, its hordes of illiterate children, its lonely and its poor in their hovels."[35] Indeed, Nano Nagle was to Cork in the eighteenth century what Mother Theresa was to Calcutta in our day.

When Dr. Moylan commended the new congregation to the Archbishop of Dublin in 1788 (some four years after Nano's death), he could say: "To the charitable exertions of that pious foundation we are principally indebted for whatever religion and morality remain among the lower class of our people."[36] But let us not think that all this was achieved without the cross of misunderstanding and even condemnation. Not only did some

Catholics misrepresent her work in the beginning, "Malignant critics . . . upbraided her for her throngs of beggars' brats! She was cursed in the streets as an impostor and her schools were derided as seminaries of vice"[37]—even of prostitution. Enduring these trials in silence, Nano spoke of them only when she felt it was her duty to let the young ladies who chose to follow her know that similar humiliations would be theirs.

Faith, Humility, and Trust in Divine Providence

Nano's faith was the wellspring of all her work. All her success was referred to God. In a letter of July 17, 1769, she says, "I began in a poor, humble manner, and although it pleased the Divine Will to give me severe trials in this foundation, yet it is to show that it is His work and has not been affected by human means."[38] In a letter of September 28, 1770, she writes:

> I had little reason when first I thought of this Foundation (Ursuline) to expect the success it has already met. I must say, every disappointment we have already had, the Almighty has been pleased to make it turn out to our advantage. . . . There is nothing in my power I shan't endeavour to do. And I hope you'll be so good as to . . . consider we are in a country in which we can't do as we please. By degrees, with the assistance of God, we may do a great deal.[39]

Referring to the Ursuline Foundation, she says in a letter of December 17, 1770: "It's all in the power of the Almighty; we don't know what is best for us and so ought to be resigned to the Divine Will." With reference to a candidate's love of teaching in the poor schools, she says in the same letter: "It shows a particular call from the great God to take delight in it."[40] With reference to the beginnings of her own congregation which she had been considering for the two years since the Ursuline Foundation was made, and she discovered her poor could not be taken care of by them, she says in a letter of September 29, 1776, "What made me defer all this time was finding myself so improper a person to undertake it. The Almighty makes use of the weakest means to bring about His works."[41] Again with reference to her own congregation, she says in a letter of August 21, 1777: "We have been under many disagreeable circumstances since we began, too tedious to mention. Yet with the Divine assistance, I think I have reason to imagine that in a few years, when we are settled, it will succeed very well."[42]

"The Zeal of Thy House Hath Eaten Me Up"

Vatican II, in its *Decree on the Apostolate of the Laity*, exhorted that: "The young should become the first apostles of the young, in direct contact with them, exercising the apostolate by themselves among themselves. . . ."[43] Two hundred years before this we find Nano Nagle writing: "All my children are brought up to be fond of instructing as I think it lies in the power of the poor to be of more service that way than the rich." Thanks to the great charity of some gentlemen who realized her pupils were well instructed, she was able to send boys to the West Indies where the Faith was in danger of being lost because the Irish emigrants were grossly ignorant of their religion when they left Ireland. She says in the same letter: "These children promise me they will take great pains with the little blacks to instruct them." Apparently, this project was to be a continuous one, for she adds: "Next year I will have pictures for them that go to give the Negroes who learn the Catechism."[44] A far cry indeed from the "beggars' brats" which this "impostor" had in her "seminaries of vice"! Nano's apostolic yearnings knew no bounds. She writes in the very first of her extant letters—1769:

> For I can assure you my schools are beginning to be of service to a great many parts of the world. This is a place of such trade; they are heard of, and my views are not for one object alone. If I could be of any service in saving souls in any part of the globe, I would willingly do all in my power.[45]

From the beginning, Nano wanted only the best educational advantages for her pupils. At different times in her letters to Miss Fitzsimmons, who was preparing in Paris to become an Ursuline for the Irish foundation, we find evidence of this. "I must say," she writes, "that I was desirous they would learn what was proper to teach young ladies hereafter, as there is a general complaint both in this kingdom and in England that the children are taught only to say their prayers."[46] (Her own schools at the time were following the curriculum used in the "little schools" of France.) In another letter she writes: "if it could be permitted them (two novices training to be Ursulines for the Irish mission) to have anybody teach them anything you thought would be an advantage hereafter to the house, don't spare any expense."[47] Just the year before the Sisters returned to Ireland she writes: "I hope that you and my cousin will get a person to instruct you in what may be useful to teach hereafter."[48] She wanted her teachers to have the best preparation possible for the teaching apostolate. It is not surprising, therefore, to find that her Sisters imbibed deeply of her continuing concern for quality education. Proof of this is found in a report of 1826 from the Commissioners of Education—men not in sympathy with Catholic education. Speaking of Presentation schools in general they could say:

> We have visited these schools and found them well conducted with great order and regularity and the children well disciplined and supplied with necessary books and school requisites. The nuns are the teachers and devote themselves to the duty of instruction with the most unwearied assiduity and attention. We were much impressed with the appearance of affection and respect on the part of the pupils towards their teachers, which characterizes those institutions to a remarkable degree. No other schools are so well attended — the moral influence of the nuns and the solicitous care exhibited by them for the education and welfare of the poor children have attracted many children of the destitute classes who would otherwise attend no school; where established, the nuns have a moral influence beyond expectation.[49]

We have further evidence of Nano's zeal in one of her several letters to Miss Mullaly who was doing a similar work in Dublin and who had requested Sisters. She writes on August 21, 1777:

> If it is the will of the Almighty, you may rely on us that every assistance in our power we shall give towards having an establishment of this Society in the Metropolis; not that I think they are so much

wanting there, only the good they do would be more universally known and extend them in other parts of the Kingdom.[50]

The next year she writes again to Miss Mulally:

I am in hopes that . . . the Almighty won't take you to himself till you see our rule established in your city, as I think none can tend more to His honor and glory in the world than it does.

It must have indeed pained her then to add:

I wish it was in my power to do what you proposed to me and I should readily have undertaken it. But I am so much involved in debt . . . you must imagine . . . how little I am at present in a situation of making a foundation in Dublin; I can hardly at present support the one I have here.[51]

Sister Rosaria O'Callaghan, PBVM, points out in her biography of Nano Nagle, *Flame of Love*, that it was not until 1794–95—ten years after Nano's death—that Miss Mullaly finally got four Sisters from Cork, thus beginning the Dublin Foundation. Sister Rosaria further notes that it was in Dublin, the Holy Week of 1800, that the Sisters first wore the religious dress in public. The Cork convents soon followed this trend. Due to the fearful penal laws, it would have been too risky to do so up to this time. (It is interesting to note here, too, that when the Sisters came to Newfoundland (1833) they were called "Mrs."— a carry-over from penal days, which continued for some years.)

Heaven Welcomes a Saint

This great lady, the foundress of our congregation of Sisters of the Presentation of the Blessed Virgin Mary, died April 26, 1784, just nine years after she founded this new Religious family. Up to April 20, she had taught daily in the schools. In fact, she collapsed on her way that morning. She tried to force herself on but had to rest in the house of a friend, where she took a severe hemorrhage. Carried back to the convent, she lingered on for five days, becoming further weakened by additional hemorrhages. Her last advice to her Sisters gathered around her was characteristic of her great love of Charity and union: "Love one another as you have hitherto done."[52] Passing on the running of the Institute to Sister Angela Collins, she asked her to be kind to those committed to her care. Union and charity were always strong points with Nano. In a letter of December 1770 addressed to one of the Ursulines in formation in Paris, she had written: "I think there is no greater happiness in the world than to be in union. Whoever we live with we must expect to have something to suffer as this world is not to be our paradise."[53]

The following gives us a glimpse into Nano's own suffering:

> What suffering was brought to light as the Sisters prepared her body for burial! Not only had disease ravaged her lungs but both knees were found to have been long in a state of massive ulceration. Yet on Holy Thursday night, just a few weeks before, she spent eleven hours on her knees in prayer before the Blessed Sacrament, as she was accustomed to do

on Holy Thursday. In addition, the soles of her feet held large and angry callouses. It was inconceivable how she had stood, not to speak of all the walking which her daily routine entailed.[54]

Nano had asked to be buried in a public cemetery. The Ursulines overruled her wishes after she died and insisted that she share their cemetery. Her Sisters acceded to their wishes. Walsh relates an interesting point in connection with her burial:

> Under penal legislation the licence of the Protestant Bishop was required to conduct a Catholic burial ceremony. The permission was not sought. A door was made in the northeastern angle of the cemetery wall which gave access to the Ursuline plot. Very quietly the mortal remains of Nano Nagle were laid in the tomb which stood against the boundary wall between the two convents.[55]

As in life, so in death! (One hundred years later the remains were removed to the cemetery of the Presentation Sisters at South Presentation Convent, Cork.) The *Hibernan Chronicle* of April 26, 1784, carried the following obituary notice:

> Last Wednesday the indisposition of Miss Nagle was announced in the sorrowing countenances of the poor of this city to whom she was the best of benefactors and patronesses. She died this day about noon and truly indescribable is the extreme of universal lamentation for the departure of a lady possessed of all that merit which for many years rendered her the object of unexampled admiration and acquired her the most unlimited esteem of all ranks of people.[56]

It is important to recall that Nano spent only nine years of her life as a consecrated religious. For more than twenty years she lived and worked as a laywoman, truly dedicated to spiritual works among the very poor.

Profile of Nano Nagle

She was a woman who, in her simplicity,
Yet dared greatly;
. . . dared to let herself be guided
by the Spirit of God. And when He,
like some will-o'-the'whisp on the mountains,
led her from the warmth of what was safe and comfortable,
out past the four walls of what was "enough" and "reasonable,"
away beyond the security of the familiar, tried and proven,
she followed with laughter in her heart.
For she had caught a glimpse of the Divine delight in reversing human logic in drawing power from weakness,
wisdom from folly,
life from death.
In this lay her strength,
This is Nano Nagle.

Sister M. Raphael Consedine, pbvm
(Victoria, Melbourne, Australia.)

Conclusion

A pillar of fire to youth and a shining light of Divine charity,[57] Nano Nagle was indeed a pioneer of Catholic education in Ireland's darkest days. Truly "everything seemed to have been lost until Nano Nagle set to work single-handedly to save the heritage of faith for childhood."[58] "Saving the heritage of faith" was truly the whole thrust of Nano Nagle's work. Her goal was aimed at the basic core of Christian education, namely, the bringing of Christ to birth in the soul of each child, as St. Paul says: "I must go through the pain of giving birth to you all over again until Christ is formed in you."[59]

It was the inspiration of Nano Nagle that gave courage and confidence to those great Irish religious educators who followed in the trail which she had blazed. Walsh comments thus:

> The religious and educational realism of Nano Nagle, her energy of planning and execution, were indispensable precedent to those who followed: Brother Edmund Rice (Founder of the Irish Christian Brothers), Mother Catherine McAuley (Foundress of the Sisters of Mercy), and Mother Theresa Ball (Foundress of the Irish Sisters of Charity).[60]

Nano Nagle accomplished something more. Her work proclaimed loudly and clearly the truth that education belongs first and foremost to the family and to the Church. The hundreds of Presentation schools scattered through Ireland, England, Australia and New Zealand, India, Pakistan, Africa, and South and North America are a massive vindication of the right of the Church to teach.

Nano Nagle counts among the numerous religious founders and Christian educators spoken of by Pius XI when he wrote:

> What of the founders of so many social and charitable institutions, of the vast numbers of saintly educators, men and women, who have perpetuated and multiplied their life work by leaving after them prolific institutions of Christian education, in aid of families and for the inestimable advantage of nations?[61]

Mother Angela Collins, Nano's successor in the Institute, wrote two years after Nano's death:

> We have the comfort to know from the best divines in the city that there never was so much good done since St. Patrick's time as has been promoted by our holy Foundress' establishments, as they say it's the only counterpoise to the Charter schools.[62]

Indeed, the author of *Lantern Beams* tells us that Nano (now Sister Mary John of God, her religious name) and her three religious sisters were strikingly successful in their work. Indeed, so much so that it was said it might not be good for the Sisters to know the vast extent of what they were affecting. On seeing the self-sacrificing devotion of the Sisters to the poor and the sick, a local doctor exclaimed: "If Almighty God never made Heaven He would do so for the Nuns of the Presentation Convent."[63] When the then reigning Pontiff, Pius VI, approved the new institute, he praised God that "in the midst of infidelity and moral depravity which prevailed in Europe, the Spirit of the Saints had found a refuge and home in Ireland."[64]

Nano's contemporary, Dr. Coppinger, wrote that "Ireland would remember Nano as "an evergreen of virtue in the vineyard of the poor, ever budding, ripening, flourishing in the young, ever mature, venerable, and productive in the old."[65] Verily, her apostolate was the "vineyard of the poor." As early as 1776, the year following the founding of the Institute, the Annals of the first convent contain this entry, which I quoted earlier: "She (Nano) intended its members to be devoted solely to works of Charity among the poor; and, in fine, to seek them out in their hovels of misery and want and woe." The author of *Lantern Beams* expresses this very beautifully when she writes:

> To Patrick God gave the task of planting the Faith in Ireland; to Nano Nagle He gave the work of rekindling its dying flame. As Patrick brought the Faith from France "The Eldest Daughter of the Church," to France Nano Nagle went to get her lantern replenished with its fires so that she might shed its beams not only in Cork but on the whole of Ireland's Spiritual Empire all over the world, because from it the faith in Ireland gained strength through her daughters and their pupils, and as they increased they travelled with the Faith to every country in the world.[66]

Did Nano Nagle envision the extent of the kingdom she was establishing for Christ? We do not know. But this we do know: she aimed at a world apostolate with every fibre of her great soul on fire with love of Christ.

The renowned Dominican preacher, Very Rev. Thomas Burke, O.P., in a sermon, delivered on the occasion of the centenary of the founding of the Presentation Congregation, spoke thus of Nano, our saintly foundress:

> A Debora appeared before the eyes of our people, and her name is in our minds and upon our lips. . . . The ferocious and brutal laws of King William III and Queen Anne were set in motion. Under penalty of banishment, fine, confiscation or imprisonment, a Catholic in Ireland — man, woman, or child — was forbidden to teach or to be taught. Nano Nagle is the Debora who turned the tide, the woman who took up the lance that had fallen from amongst forty thousand in Israel. She is the woman whom God chose and whom He raised up to be the mother of that Irish Catholic education which has preserved our faith, preserved the glory of the purity and morality of our Irish womanhood, which has sent us forth to the ends of the earth to be apostles to nations, and which has delivered the greatest victory of Ireland's faith and apostleship over the powers of darkness. Such was this woman. [67]

Nano Nagle, you who were another Brigid, another Debora, a second St. Patrick, a torchbearer in some of the most turbulent days of Ireland's history, we, your Sisters in Newfoundland and Labrador, salute your Herculean labours for the young, the sick, the poor, and the sorrowing—the weak and the needy! To us in the twenty-first century the torch has been passed. May we ever hold it high as we follow in your footsteps, spurred on by your spirit of deep faith, dogged perseverance, and abiding trust in God.

Jerome Kiely in the following poem spells out quite well the conditions under which Nano worked:

NANO NAGLE

The streets were trenches flowing with despair
Into a redder Nile than Moses smote,
And darkness smothered laughter in the throat
and hunched the heart beneath a sky of care,
When she came wings-a-cloak down Bethel stair
To wicker infant hopes in prayer and float them
Godwards, and on every door she wrote
With blood her lantern pulsed "This people spare."

Lanes her hem touched were cured of hopelessness:
Her cloak was motherskirt that cuddled crowds,
And desert tent for hearts loveparched and stray.
Her lamp swung on a door to happiness,
Brought life to minds were nurtured in their shrouds
And showed the way to light was Light, the Way.[68]

Sister Angela Curtis, PBVM, in her scholarly paper on Nano Nagle, uses a poem by one of Ireland's most loved and distinguished poets—Gerald Griffin. I can think of no more thought-provoking way to close this piece of research on our loved foundress than to quote this poem:

THE LADY OF THE LANTERN

Is no waking reserved for our sleep of despair?
O see! There's a shooting of light in the gloom
And the spirit of Nano replies from the tomb.
Hail, Star of the lowly! Apostle of light!
In the glow of whose fervour the cottage grew bright.
Sweet violet of Sanctity, lurking concealed
Till the wind wafts the leaf and the bloom is revealed.
By the light of that glory which burst on thy youth
In its daytime of pleasure, and woke it to truth;
By the tears thou hast shed, by the toil thou hast borne.
Oh say, shall our night know no breaking of morn?[69]

II

The Coming of the Presentation Sisters to Newfoundland

Excerpts From the Writings of
Sister Mary James Dinn, PBVM, MA

Beyond the possible !
New expressions of Presentation mission

Presentation Sisters in Newfoundland

The following section is part of an historical publication: *Foundation of the Presentation Congregation in
Newfoundland*. This fine piece of writing—of which I am
quoting some sections, verbatim and quite freely—was done
by one of our Newfoundland Sisters, Sister Mary James
Dinn (a former Superior General) to commemorate the
bicentennial, in 1976, of the founding of the Sisters of the
Presentation in Cork, Ireland.

Bishop Fleming Brings Presentation Sisters to Newfoundland[70]

It was Bishop Michael Anthony Fleming (1830–1850)—a Franciscan—who gave such an impetus to religion and to Catholic education in the Island that whatever success attended future efforts can be traced back to his initiative. He was appointed Vicar-Apostolic of Newfoundland and Bishop of Carpasia *in partibus* in 1829, the year in which the British Emancipation Act recognized the rights of Catholics. Following his appointment, his first work was to procure priests from the Old World. His objective was to establish a pastor in every place where one could be supported. After he had obtained sixteen priests and had placed them in various parts of the island, he was convinced that the next essential step was to establish a religious order in Newfoundland and to ensure a Catholic education for the Catholic children.

Having given a concise and quite interesting account of public education in Newfoundland at this time, Sister James continues:

In 1833 Bishop Fleming went to Ireland for the purpose of visiting the Presentation Convent in Galway which seemed to him to be the most likely place to obtain volunteers for his mission, as the superior of the convent there—Mother John Power—was a native of Waterford with which place many of the Irish in Newfoundland had ties of relationship and friendship. On June 29, he approached Mother John with his request for Sisters, telling her of the conditions in his territory, of his great concern for the children in his charge, and of the urgent need for Religious Sisters who would train the youth of the Island to become truly Christian, so that these would in turn train others. When Mother John placed his request before the assembled community, the response was immediate. Sister Magdalen O'Shaughnessy was the first volunteer for the New World, followed after a few moments by Sister Xaverius Lynch, just a few months professed. Then Sister Mary Bernard Kirwin, bursar of the Galway community, made a third volunteer; then there was a fourth—Sister Mary Xavier Maloney—who was then fifty-one years old.

It is interesting to note here that, according to our archives, these brave and courageous women were bilingual (French and English) and all highly educated. In addition to business education, they were prepared to teach all the fine arts—painting, as well as piano, violin, harp, and, of course, voice. A very beautiful oil painting of Our Blessed Lady hangs on the wall above the mantelpiece in the drawing room at our Motherhouse, Cathedral Square, St. John's. It is the work of a Miss Pendergast (Harbour Grace), a pupil of Sister Xaverius Lynch.

> Bishop Fleming, filled with gratitude, sincerely thanked Mother John and the four Sisters and he immediately went to seek the consent of Dr. Brown, the Bishop of Galway. Naturally, Bishop Brown was very surprised and he expressed great concern for the welfare of those Sisters who had volunteered. However, he gave his consent and his blessing to this new venture. Preparations for their departure began. The four volunteers made their eight-day retreat which normally took place during

the summer holidays, and Bishop Fleming began to make arrangements for passage to Newfoundland. Some years earlier, Bishop Scallan had bequeathed to Bishop Fleming £1,500 for his mission and this amount he now appropriated to the Newfoundland foundation with a guarantee of another hundred pounds annually for the support of the Sisters, and with the promise that in due time he would build a suitable convent and school for them. Mother Power and her advisors agreed to these terms but made the stipulation that the Galway community would be empowered to recall the Sisters after six years of service if they wished to return.

Woman of Global Vision

"If I could be of service in saving souls in any part of the globe, I would willingly do all in my power."
— Nano Nagle

The Lord has carried us along the road we have travelled and so we celebrate His faithfulness, continuing our journey with trust in His Fatherly care.

(Deut. 1:30)

Arrival in St. John's, Newfoundland

On August 12, 1833, the four Sisters left Galway for Waterford from where on August 28 they, accompanied by the Bishop, embarked on the brig "Ariel." After a voyage of twenty-five days on the ocean, they arrived in St. John's harbour on September 21. An excerpt from the newspaper "Newfoundlander" has the following editorial:

ARRIVAL OF RIGHT REVEREND DR. FLEMING: On Saturday morning, September 21, this respected Prelate arrived in the brig "Ariel" after a short passage from Waterford. On the previous day, the brig "Cabinet" arrived from Waterford with five clergymen for this mission; both vessels were released from quarantine at the same time. . . . At twelve o'clock His Lordship and the Religious Ladies landed and were received amidst the most vehement and enthusiastic cheering. Dr. Carson politely provided his carriage for the Nuns in which they were conveyed to the Episcopal residence.

In the newspaper just mentioned, there is another item as follows:

The Ladies, who in their zeal for religion have expatriated themselves from their native country, are the Presentation Order of Nuns—a society whose lives are entirely devoted to the imparting to children of the humbler classes in society useful education combined with religious instruction.[71]

The names of the four Sisters are then listed. Thus did the first Presentation Sisters set foot on the soil of the New World. (They were also the first

English speaking Sisters in what is now Canada.) A section of the Bishop's residence had been set aside for them where they lived for a month.

In letters to Mother John Power dated September 22, 1833, the day following their arrival in St. John's, the Sisters gave detailed accounts of their voyage of over three weeks, of the storms encountered, of the sea-sickness suffered, and finally of their arrival in St. John's on the feast of St. Matthew. To quote from one of Sister Magdalen's letters:

> We arrived on the 21st September, the feast of St. Matthew. All the population of the town flocked down to the wharves, and climbed up the masts of the vessels to see us and to welcome us; and some of the principal inhabitants came on board, vying with each other for the honor of rowing us ashore. We were not allowed to disembark until they had made a new landing stair. The best carriage in the town was sent to fetch us.[72]

These letters got mislaid in Liverpool, and no account of their arrival in Newfoundland was received at the convent in Galway for four months. The community gave them up as lost. Solemn requiem Masses were celebrated for them, copies of their vows were burned, and a period of mourning was observed in the convent in Galway.

Opening of the First Presentation School in Newfoundland

Within a month after their arrival, the Sisters took up their abode in a residence which had been renovated for them. It had formerly been a tavern with the name of "The Rising Sun," a name which the townsfolk considered to be a propitious omen, symbolizing the light of faith and education which the Sisters came to diffuse throughout the country. On October 21, they opened their first school where 450 children were waiting to be admitted. Archbishop Howley says that "never was there witnessed in St. John's a scene of deeper interest than the opening of the Presentation school."[73] In reporting this event, a local newspaper — The "Patriot" — edited by a Protestant — carried the following editorial:

> Seldom has it been our lot to witness a scene of such deep interest, . . . whether we regard the community of ladies surrendering all the joys of life for the advancement of the glory of Him to whom they have consecrated their lives, or the little applicant for admission, . . . or the multitudinous feelings of the estimable Prelate to whose exertions we owe this blessing. There he stood, witnessing the completion of his dearest wishes.[74]

The accommodations which this building afforded were insufficient for such a large enrolment. Notwithstanding the fact that the Sisters reserved for themselves only two bedrooms and a parlour which served as chapel, common room, and refectory, they could not house the ever-increasing numbers. Although Dr. Fleming had rented this place for one year, he immediately set about procuring a larger building. He rented a house which formerly had been the residence of the Anglican Archdeacon of St. John's and fitted it up as a convent. On December 8 of the same year, the Sisters moved into it, and there they remained for nine years, giving the locality the name "Nunnery Hill"—a name which it bears to this day. The Bishop then undertook the building of a large convent and school on Long's Hill. In August 1843, not wishing to renew the lease on the house on Nunnery Hill, Bishop Fleming arranged for the Sisters to move to a house which had been a ball-alley, situated a little outside the town. In December 1844 they took possession of the beautiful new convent on Long's Hill, just completed at a cost of £4,000.

In the meantime, two postulants had joined the original four—Catherine Phelan from New Ross, County Wexford, and Amelia Shanley from Dublin . . . But six Sisters could not cope with the daily attendance of over 1,000 pupils, even though these Sisters were trained to work with large numbers. So once again Bishop Fleming made an appeal to the Galway convent for volunteers for the Newfoundland mission.

The appeal was successful and two more Sisters from the Galway community volunteered. They were Sister M. Josephine French, Superior of the Galway community, and Sister Mary de Sales Lovelock, Novice Mistress.

On June 9, 1846, when the greater part of the city of St. John's was destroyed by fire, the new convent and school were burned. Bishop Fleming was still in Ireland and when he received the tragic news, he offered to release from their promise the two Sisters who had recently volunteered for his mission and who were then actually at Liverpool awaiting passage to St. John's. But in spite of the news of the destruction caused by the fire and Bishop Fleming's offer to release them, they were determined to persevere in their decision to join their Sisters in St. John's, now in dire distress. The latter, now homeless, had taken refuge in the Bishop's small country cottage about a mile outside of town. The Sisters of Mercy (who had arrived in 1842) had invited them to remain with them until a house could be provided, but they did not wish to give them trouble. Also, many of the townspeople had offered to take them into their homes but the Sisters refused all offers as they were living a somewhat cloistered life since the approval of their rules and constitutions in 1805. They remained at the Bishop's cottage during the next five months, teaching the children on fine days in the open fields, and in rough weather in the stables and barns. It is said that when Dr. Fleming arrived in St. John's and beheld the complete destruction of the city and saw the new convent and school reduced to ashes, he never fully recovered from the shock. Certainly from that time on, his health began to decline. In November he arranged for the Sisters to live in a part of the Mercy Convent and he erected a temporary school for them nearby. Here they remained for five years.

As editor of Sister James's work, I wish to add a note. Our archives tell us that in the fire of 1846, the Long's Hill convent and the school had escaped the conflagration of the city, as the fire had not reached that area. However, the Sisters had opened their doors to the fire's victims to store their belongings and bits of furniture, among which were smouldering embers. In the night the whole place was ablaze. The Sisters barely escaped with their lives—victims of their own charity.

Following an account of Bishop Fleming's immediate plans for a new convent and school that, due to his sickness and subsequent death, had to be postponed until 1850, Sister James continues with her interesting account of our early Sisters in Newfoundland.

Presentation Motherhouse, St. John's, Newfoundland, Built in 1853. School on the right.

New Presentation Convent and School

On August 23, 1850, Bishop Mullock, who succeeded Bishop Fleming, laid the foundation of a new Presentation Convent and School on a beautiful site close to the Cathedral. On October 21, 1851 — the anniversary of the opening of their first school eighteen years previously — the Sisters moved from the Mercy convent and took up their abode in a portion of the unfinished new school. On July 2, 1853, they took formal possession of their new convent and school erected at a cost of £7,000. This convent is now the Motherhouse of the Presentation Congregation in Newfoundland. This was the eighth house they had occupied since their arrival in 1833. At that time, there were nine professed religious in the community in St. John's, twenty in outlying places, and several novices and postulants. There is a memo dated 1855 in Bishop Mullock's handwriting which states:

> In the diocese of Newfoundland at the present 30 priests, John T. Mullock, Bishop, 5 Presentation Convents, 1 Convent of the Sisters of Mercy, Catholics about 65,000 or 70,000, Chapels 62. St. John's, 1855.[75]

Spread of the Presentation Congregation Throughout Newfoundland

By this time new branches of the Order had been founded outside St. John's, the first of these having been established in the town of Harbour Grace on July 1, 1851.

On Monday, July 7, they opened their first school. In addition to pupils of regular school age, girls of twenty years of age and over joyfully availed themselves of this opportunity for education, both religious and secular. The Sisters also conducted Sunday school classes for both children and adults. All the women of the town assembled on Sundays for religious instruction, and girls who could not attend school on week days were taught reading and writing at these Sunday classes.

It was in this way that, despite their Rule of Enclosure at

that time, the Sisters found ways of reaching out to the wider community as our Foundress, Nano Nagle, had so lovingly done.

Having described successive Presentation foundations in Carbonear, Fermeuse (later moved to Renews), Sister James notes that during the next decade six foundations were made, one in St. John's West (St. Patrick's Convent) and the others in nearby settlements in the diocese of St. John's. She then gives some pertinent facts about the opening of the convents in Harbour Breton (later moved to St. Jacques), Stephenville (the first in a number of convents on the west coast of Newfoundland), then Corner Brook in 1927, and then Grand Falls in 1933, the first of the three convents in Central Newfoundland.

The next forty years saw some thirty more convents established throughout the island, with one in Toronto, Ontario, and one in Davis Inlet, Labrador. In the early 1990s two houses were established in the West Indies: one in Dominica and one in Antigua.

Next we find an account of the amalgamation of all the convents in 1916 in order to promote, through centralization, greater efficiency in the work of the Congregation and greater temporal and spiritual advantages for the Sisters. Sister James next talks about the history of the Rules and Constitution and the revisions after Vatican II, those of the Chapter of Affairs in 1968 and the new and final draft that was drawn up by our 1979 Chapter of Affairs.

The section of Sister James's book entitled *Specific Contribution to Education* gives us very interesting information on the Government's involvement in education. Noting that in the area of the training of teachers the Presentation Sisters played an important part, she continues:

The first contribution of the Government for the purpose of teacher training was made by the Act of 1853. In this Act no reference is made to the training of Roman Catholic teachers (a definite denominational system of education was not set out until the Act of 1874). Dr. Fred Rowe in his book *The Development of Education in Newfoundland* gives the following explanation:

. . . much of the Catholic teaching was being done by members of the religious orders, the majority of whom were well trained in Ireland before coming out to Newfoundland. . . . later the convents undertook to train female teachers for Roman Catholic schools, although the actual date when this work started is not clear. From statements made by Bishop Mullock and others, it is likely that it started very soon after the establishment of the Orders in Newfoundland.[76]

The following excerpts from REPORT UPON THE INSPECTION OF CATHOLIC SCHOOLS FOR THE YEAR 1862, signed by Michael John Kelly — one of the first school inspectors in the Island — support the statement that the Presentation Sisters were at that time training female lay teachers:

. . . The Lamaline school is closed, and will continue so until a school house is erected there, when a trained teacher from the Presentation Convent, St. John's, will take charge of it.[77]

And speaking of the District of Placentia West, the inspector reports:

I found the schools in this district progressing favourably. Two trained female teachers from the Presentation Convent, St. John's, had charge of two of the schools, namely, Presque and Merasheen, and were conducting them very satisfactorily. [The Sisters in Placentia also trained girls for schools in Placentia Bay].[78]

In 1864, a questionnaire was sent to all school boards in Newfoundland requesting their comments regarding the training of teachers for the schools in the island. Bishop Mullock, replying as Chairman of the Roman Catholic School Board for St. John's, expressed satisfaction with the progress being made. An excerpt from his reply is given below:

Our training system for teachers is as good as I have found in any country I am acquainted with. The teachers have all the advantages of the College School, and the mental training and discipline after school hours necessary to qualify them for the future position. . . . The Nuns train free of expense any number of female teachers who present themselves, and we generally send teachers to the outports from the St. John's convent schools.[79]

The Act of 1892 recognized the following institutions as qualified to undertake the training of teachers:

The Roman Catholic College (males), Presentation Convent (females), Church of England College, Central Training School of the Newfoundland School Society, Methodist College, General

Protestant College, and the Congregational Training School.[80]

In the concluding remarks to her fine piece of history, Sister Mary James made this very apropos statement:

> It is one hundred and forty-two years, [actually at this date—2006—it is one hundred and seventy-three years], since those brave Sisters from the Galway community volunteered their assistance in the cause of religion and Catholic education in Newfoundland. It is difficult, in fact well-nigh impossible, to evaluate the work and the contribution to the Church made by any religious Order. The historian may attempt to reconstruct the pattern traced out through generations past and may even endeavour to predict the ways of the future, but only the Divine Master can appraise the true value of the undertakings and accomplishments of any individual or group. From a study of the history of the Church in Canada, as elsewhere, it is clear that God seems to endow founders and foundresses with souls of tempered steel, for no setbacks ever daunt them or turn them from their noble purposes. The oak tree is the emblem of the Presentation Congregation, and as new trees spring from acorns that fall from the parent tree, so have new foundations of the Presentation Congregation sprung up in numerous countries of the world.[81]

Let me conclude this splendid piece of research by Sister Mary James by saying that Nano Nagle's spirit indeed flowed over into the Sisterhood she founded. We find Bishop Fleming, O.S.F., writing from Newfoundland a few years after the arrival of the Sisters here:

Upwards of 4,000 children have passed through their hands; there is scarcely a spot in the Island where their pupils may not be found, giving the greatest edification.[82]

Years later, before retiring from active labour, this great Bishop of Catholic emancipation in Newfoundland wrote to a friend in Ireland:

> And so the good work goes on. Hundreds, nay thousands, are annually sent forth from their schools trained in the highest principles of virtue and honesty, conferring on our country a blessing incomparably rich, and producing a race of mothers of families such as Newfoundland may be proud of.[83]

The year of 2006 marks the one hundred and seventy-third year since, as Sister Mary James put it, "those brave Sisters from Galway community volunteered their assistance in the cause of Catholic education in Newfoundland."

Sisters Magdalen O'Shaughnessy, Xaverius Lynch, Mary Bernard Kirwin, and Mary Xavier Maloney, to you, the first Sisters to come to our Island, hail! We reverently cherish your shining example and acclaim your fortitude and courage in cradling our congregation in Newfoundland. Sailing from Galway you were the first of our Sisters to brave the treacherous ocean, and face the unknown in a strange land—the first Presentation Sisters to set foot in the New World as you volunteered to bring Christ to the children of the Irish emigrants in Newfoundland. May your undaunted courage, your unconditional dedication, your undying spirit of sacrifice ever continue to inspire us and lead many young ladies to follow in your footsteps.

Today our Presentation Sisters are found in colleges, renewal centres, hospitals, parishes, and almost any office requiring pastoral dimension. Communally and individually, they strive to live out Nano's charism in teaching, healing, and caring for the People of God.

Following Sister Mary James's account of the coming of the Presentation Sisters to Newfoundland and the present editor's closing remarks, I leave you with the following lines from Sister Miriam Martin's latest musical composition, *Fire to the Rock*:

> *Four women cross waters,*
> *New worlds to behold;*
> *From fragile beginnings*
> *The good seeds are sown,*
> *And Newfoundland shores*
> *Presentation's new home.*

The First Presentation Sisters In North America

From Galway to Newfoundland

LETTERS WRITTEN TO THE CONVENT IN GALWAY, IRELAND

To Rev. Mother, Presentation Convent, Galway, by the foundress when the sisters arrived in Newfoundland on September 21, 1833.

> St. John's
> Newfoundland
> September 22nd, 1833

My ever dear Revd. Mother,

I am sure you will be delighted to hear we are at last arrived at St. John's after a most unpleasant voyage of 25 days. I will endeavour to give you as exact an account as I can of it. We left Waterford on the 20th August. We were only a few hours on board when we all got sick and were obliged to go to our berths. We were almost insensible. Any expressions I can make use of could give you but a faint idea of Dr. Fleming's kindness and attention. Nothing was left undone which could in any way contribute to our comfort. On the third day after we left Ireland we had a storm. One of the masts was broken and some others damaged. It lasted for three days but we were not much frightened because, almost regardless of what was going on, we were so deadly sick, but we soon had another storm to encounter which was most awful. It was on the 10th. It lasted 36 hours. As for myself, I did not lose my confidence all this time. I had a feeling almost amounting to certainty that God would not abandon us and as we left all those we so fondly loved for love of Him, this encouraged me to hope, I may say even against hope. The vessel became unmanageable so that the crew could no longer work and in such cases they think it better to let her trust to the mercy of the wind and waves. This was in the evening, so, my dear Rev. Mother, you may fancy what a night we passed. I often thought of the secure and comfortable home our dear Sisters enjoyed but I must acknowledge at the same time I did not regret for a moment the step we had taken. The storm soon ceased and we got on until we came in view of land. We were in great spirits thinking we could go on shore in a short time, but we met another disappointment: heavy fogs and contrary winds prevented us from landing and we were for three days tossed about within a few miles of St. John's.

(Excerpt from a letter of Sister Magdalen
O'Shaughnessy)

My dearest Rev. Mother: I need scarcely tell you what a happiness it is for me to be able to write to you and my dear Community and be assured though separated from you and my dear Sisters, that my heart and affections are still with you. We arrived in the harbour of St. John's 6 o'clock Friday morning, September 21st, and as soon as there was intimation of the Bishop having arrived, there were crowds of people coming on board to see him at that early hour, for we could not go on shore until we underwent an inspection of the officers of health, who indeed complimented the Bishop by coming out at an early hour which they were unaccustomed to, for they generally leave the people in the harbour until ten or eleven o'clock. They came in a small boat and we just stood at the side of the vessel; they barely looked at us and said very politely that was sufficient. Nothing could equal the delight of the people at the Bishop's return: they had the greatest preparations for him. Before we left the vessel, there was an address presented to him by the members of Parliament and early in the morning the people assembled in the chapel that they might have a procession to receive him. It was a most grand sight. We crossed the harbour in a small boat and when we came near the shore there were crowds of small boats full of people; the banks and hills were crowded and as soon as the boat that the bishop and we were in arrived there was nothing to be heard but shouts of joy and acclamations. Our ears were stunned with the noise and cries of: "You're welcome, my Lord and may you live long." All hats were off. Protestants, Orangemen and all kinds of people came to welcome us and you may guess how we felt when we found ourselves in the midst of such a concourse of people and received in the most flattering manner. Everyone was most attentive to us. As soon as we arrived, they had a carriage ready to receive us. The Bishop told us that our entry made the greatest impression on the people, so much so that several persons were dissolved to tears, even those who were, as he said, with hearts of stone, on whom he often endeavoured to make an impression. Everyone is most anxious to see us; several of the most respectable called and left their visiting cards, Protestants among the rest, but we appeared to no one until we opened school. Some pious women came into the room where we were and I was never more astonished when they threw themselves on their knees and asked our blessing and kissed our hands and welcomed us a thousand times. Indeed everything gives us hopes that with the assistance of God we will succeed.

(Excerpt from a letter from Sister Xaverius Lynch)

In 2006, 173 years have passed since those letters were written home. Sister Xaverius Lynch's expressed hope came true: God did assist those courageous women, and the Presentation Congregation spread to many parts of the Island—and beyond.

III

Celebrating Nano Nagle In Poetry
and
Poetically Finding God In All of Life

Contributions from our Sisters Appearing in our Community Newsletters
Avete and Team Topics

SEPTEMBER 21, 1833

As Nano once, across the Irish Sea,
    Heard plaintive voices calling her to come
        From France's peaceful joys and sunny scenes,
            The children's voices calling "Home! Come home!"

So did those four from Galway's gentle shore
    Hear far off voices of another band
        Of children 'cross a wilder, stormier foam
            "Come, Sisters, come to us in Newfoundland."

They came with glowing hearts, with courage high,
    With faces steadfast towards a far, dim west,
        To live, to labour through the long slow years,
            And, at God's pleasure, here at last to rest.

Scattered their ashes lie,
    To bless and sanctify this foreign loam;
        This other Ireland, 'neath an alien sky,
            This new land, that their hearts called home.

Catherine Sullivan, PBVM
Newfoundland, 1975.

TO ANY PLACE ON EARTH

To any place on earth she'd gladly go,
So said our Mother in her loving zeal,
If she could feed the message of God's Word
To hungry hearts, and help those poor hearts feel
The wonder of His love.

But she was penned in one small island's girth,
And she was compassed by her life's short span;
Still, as her longing gaze swept all the earth,
She knelt to pray, and the great work began.

Now that two hundred years have come and gone,
Her name and spirit ring this wide world round,
And we, her Sisters, gladly, humbly strive
From California, east to Pakistan
To plant a seed and keep her faith alive;
And so, in peace or strife, in joy or tears,
To sing her triumph of two hundred years.

Catherine Sullivan, PBVM
Newfoundland, 1975.

THE **Almighty** is ALL-SUFFICIENT.

1769

Mother Nagle

NANO NAGLE

Have you heard of Nano Nagle
Of Irish birth and fame,
Who founded the Presentations
For the glory of God's name?

Two hundred years have passed by
And still she walks the earth
As today her Sisters follow,
In prayer, work, song and mirth.

She left them a Gospel message:
Love God with your whole being,
Love one another truly
With the poor be always seen.

Be humble, courageous, joyful
Follow where the Spirit leads,
Take Mary as your model,
As for you she daily pleads.

The almighty is all-sufficient,
He makes use of the weakest tools,
Above all other charities
Must be the schools, the schools.

Thus did their Foundress teach them
To be strong with the strength of God,
When they pray and love and labour
As they follow the ways she trod.

May our prayer this Bi-Centennial
In Chapel or on green sod
Be "to see her soon in Heaven,
A Saint 'mong the Saints of God"

Matthew Byrne, PBVM
Newfoundland, 1975.

FAVOURITE TIME

When there's not a ripple on the water,
When the whistling of birds fills the air
That's cool and quiet after the heat
Of a summer day

When pink and white musk flowers
Bow their pretty faces till another dawn;

When shadows are lost but echoes can still be heard,
When footsteps on the sidewalk grow louder,
When there's only a wee faint glow of sunset left

It's a peace-filled moment
And it makes me aware again
Of how powerful and present
You are, Lord.
This is my favourite time.

Margie Byrne, PBVM
Newfoundland, August 1975.

Painting by
Mary K. Connolly,
2004.

THREE TREES

In the golden sunset of the crispy fall
While the flicking birds continue their call,
Amid colours of crimson, brown, yellow and gold,
With scenic background glorious to behold;
On the top of a hill "Three Trees" emerge,
Against an azure skyline where fleecy clouds converge
A narrow path meanders in the midst of this hue,
Snakelike and brown which enhances the view.

Oft in the stilly morn I gaze,
At my favourite spot while still amazed,
I think of the beauteous nature so fine,
And grieve for those who must repine;
I muse on Mother Earth who nurtures the tree,
But most of all God, I think of Thee.

Tarcisia Fewer, PBVM
Newfoundland, 1976.

(This poem was published, on Merit, by the
Poetry Institute of Canada, 1976.)

Take down your lantern from its niche and go out!
You may not rest in firelight certainties,
Secure from drifting fog of doubt and fear.
You may not build yourself confining walls
And say: "Thus far, and thus, and thus far shall I walk,
And these things shall I do, and nothing more"
Go out! For need calls loudly in the winding lanes
And you must seek Christ there.
Your pilgrim heart
Shall urge you still one pace beyond,
And love shall be your lantern flame.

Raphael Consedine, PBVM
Victoria, Australia, 1977.

(Taken from her book, *One Pace Beyond: The Life of Nano Nagle*.)

This Hymn/Song and the following two *Light for the Journey* and *Follow the Flame* come from a number of spiritual songs written and recorded in the early eighties by Miriam Martin, PBVM, Ph.D. Miriam is one of our Newfoundland Presentations who hails from Nova Scotia is presently is teaching at St. Paul's University in Ottawa.

TAKE DOWN YOUR LANTERN

Take down your lantern, the gift of Jesus Christ
You cannot stay here in quiet firelight
Take down your lantern, love is the blessed flame.
Christ shall lead your journey through foreign winding lanes.

Refrain:
Take down your lantern
Go out into the night,
In your weakness
Jesus will be your light.

Take down your lantern, let your vision guide your feet.
You cannot choose the finished, the complete.
Follow the flame of the saints you've found.
Your pilgrim heart shall urge you one pace beyond.

Take down your lantern, there's so much dark and cold,
Gaze on its beauty till its flame makes your heart bold.
Take down your lantern, it is your gift of life
And love is your purpose, the lover, Jesus Christ.

We take down our lanterns, our vision guides our feet.
We cannot choose the finished, the complete.
We follow the flame our saints have found.
Our pilgrim hearts will urge us one pace beyond.

Miriam Martin, PBVM
Newfoundland.

LIGHT FOR THE JOURNEY

Give us light for our journey, Give us light for our way.
The path is winding and dim. Turn us to fire within
Give us light, give us light.
For we have been scattered, we have been torn;
We have rejoiced and laughed. We have been reborn!

Sacrament of friendship,
Alliances of love;
Tears and fears and hopes we've shared
We've dreams to be fulfilled.

People fired with vision,
Fragile, firm and true;
Peace and Justice have embraced,
We're reconciled anew.

Miriam Martin, PBVM
Newfoundland.

FOLLOW THE FLAME

We follow the flame of the lantern
Its fire lights the way through the dark.
We follow the flame, that lights up the way
Compelled by the fire in our hearts.

We follow though often short-sighted,
Our feet find the path as we go.
O stumbling and strong we move along
With the flame of the fire in our souls.

We follow though few come behind us,
The lantern's new tracks through the night.
God's freeing reign calls, and though we are small
We still bear the flame in our hearts.

We follow the flame of the lantern
Its fire lights our way through the dark.
We follow the flame, that lights up our way
Impelled by the love in our hearts.

Come, follow the flame of the lantern
Let its fire light your way through the dark.
Come follow the flame, let it light up your way
Compelled by the love in your heart.

Come follow the flame of the lan . . . tern.

Miriam Martin, PBVM
Newfoundland.

REFLECTIONS

A Walk in the Woods
(Recollection Day, November 1988)

The sun shines bright
The sky is blue.
A blanket of fresh snow
Glimmers in my path.
I lament that it is soon to be
Graffiti marked by flat and
Sturdy boots—
Shall I be the culprit?
But nature calls,
"God's presence is in here!"
The calm and quiet of this
Haunting place
Make Him feel close.
I'm happy and at peace
No longer do I lament
The marks upon the snow,
Knowing this was meant to be.
Soon it will be freshly covered
And, like my soul—renewed.

Angela McKenzie, PBVM
Newfoundland.

A WALK IN THE WOODS

(Recollection Day, April 1989)

The sun shines bright,
The sky is blue.
The snow has gone—
Not really gone, but living still
In babbling brooks
And buds and leafy green.
My love and trust and hope
Soar high with singing birds
As, enveloped by deep peace,
His presence everywhere
Calls me to pray;
To touch, to feel the joy
That only He can share.
This too was meant to be.
Again refreshed, renewed, my heart proclaims
"My God is here!"

Angela McKenzie, pbvm
Newfoundland.

SOUNDS OF PEACE AND SILENCE

The blue-grey shadows of evening,
The soft rustling wind,
The sound of the chickadees
Singing their evening prayer
From the trees on Poplar Avenue.

Other squeaker birds in the nearby trees
Sing their praise also
Add Praise to the Creator.

The distant sounds of the Mill.
The tap, tap of a hammer in someone's back garden.

And further along the road
The stillness of the blazing sun throwing
Around the weight of its late evening glow.
It's indescribable beauty—the Peace!
I hear it in the Sounds of Peace and Silence.

Margie Byrne, PBVM
Retreat at St. Catherine's
Grand Falls–Windsor, NL, 1990.

GOOD FRIDAY, 1991

It's Good Friday!
A strange quiet pervades the air,
Workers rest, businesses close,
Traffic slows,
Creation waits in awed expectancy.

It's Good Friday!
Hearts turn inward, knees bend,
Heads bow low,
Eyes turn upward to Jesus—
Confronted—by the mystery of God's Love!

It's Good Friday!
Some stop to linger near the Cross,
Others mingle with the passers-by
And move on—
Too busy yet to stay awhile.

Good Friday!
It flashes into our consciousness,
Lights up our harried existence,
Calls us once again to look at Jesus
To hear His Word—to listen—
"Here is Love—here is Life—
I love you—I die for you."

Good Friday—Good Friday—
Echoing down the Ages!

Clotilde Meaney, PBVM
Newfoundland.

-84-

RICH DOUGH

White rising, delicate bulk, dough,
Bread making, soft, foamy mound,
Yeast infested, watered flour,
Germinating, unfolding power
In the warm quiet hour.
Clearly this panned dough
Caresses the mystery of life.
The dying of the yeast gives
Rise to the creation of the bread.
In the process of rising dough
Changing into formed loaves
I'm drawn into the reality of life.
In the unfolding of my encounters
With the passing of my relationships
My life—like the dough—dies,
Rises, transforms and prepares
For the moulding of the loaf.
May each "bun of bread"
Hold my life in Eternal stead.

Laurane Pittman, PBVM
Newfoundland, June 1992.

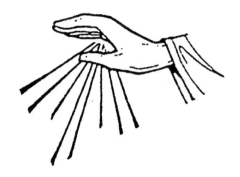

TRANSFIGURATION

Up to the mountain top went the three
Invited by Jesus to come and see.
There in the quiet out of sight
He became but a dazzling light.
Talking with Elias and Moses too
The three weren't sure just what to do.
Peter in pleading wanted to stay
To make of the place a permanent spot.
For they feared, not secure in their lot.
From out of the cloud a rich voice they heard
"This is my beloved Son, listen to His word."
Looking around all was as before
There was only Jesus—no need for more.
They left the strange place came back to save face
While they were gone life went on
The others had the work done
And they had bathed in the Son.

Laurane Pittman, PBVM
Newfoundland, Holy Thursday, 1992.

TWO LONGINGS MEET

O God within and all around
God who longs but to be found
God who waits with arms held wide
And bids me tred this holy ground.

O God, I long to hear your Word
To know your Son as only Lord
To have your Spirit set me free
And in my fear be reassured.

You gently hold my fragile shell
You take my hand: all will be well
Your faithfulness my only shield
"Come first be filled. Then go and tell!"

Your call to simply empty be
That you might set my spirit free
To cling to naught but you alone
And know how deep your love for me.

I lift my heart in grateful praise
In joyful hope my hands I raise
My listening heart like Mary's be
My journey hers these blessed days.

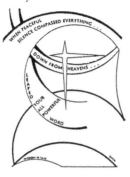

Sheila Leonard, PBVM
Newfoundland,
August 1993.

ADVENT IN JULY
(Summer Reflection)

To Mary

Love bade you journey forth; go slow
And time would yield what you'd need to know
The doing God's, yours to simply be
The rest God's will would do in Thee.

Kinswomen, friends, beloved, so dear
Your journey called, midst hardships to bear
But love persists to the journey's end
Such love would not be bound by fear.

I journeyed forth with you today
Touched deeply your joy along the way
Such awesome news could not be contained
Your Christ within: what more to say!

Such holy news, such gift Divine
By grace has stayed the passing of time
Your Christ within e'er born anew
Today I knew your gift as mine.

Teach me Mary, how to go
How to listen for what I need to know
The doing God's, mine to simply be
The rest God's love will do in me.

Sheila Leonard, PBVM
Newfoundland,
July 1994.

MY ROSE

My Rose tells me of God and love,
Its rich color, let it be pink, red or yellow,
Its fragrance, its beauty

It writes its own Gospel
Tells its own love story.

A husband gives a rose to his loved one,
A boy gives a rose to his sweetheart,
A son or daughter gives a rose to their Mother,
In a very special way they all say, "I love you."

Weddings, Anniversaries, and Birthdays
Can't go by without roses.
Even on the death of a loved one,
Roses are ever present signs of love and resurrection.

And it doesn't end in death
Every Anniversary or Birthday a rose drops by;
It may end up at a special Mass
Or perhaps on the grave of a loved one.

As life goes on, so does the beautiful Rose
Saying, "I love you dearly."
It continues to speak the everlasting love of God
As the years go by.

Mary Kennedy, PBVM
Newfoundland,
Advent Retreat, 1996.

MY MYSTICAL EXPERIENCE OF A PLAYFUL GOD

In the beginning the Word was God
There was darkness
Then the Playful God said: Let there be LIGHT
Let there be . . .
Let there be . . .
God played as He created this wonderful universe!
Last, but not least, He made us . . . woman and man.
He gave us a part of Himself
His own image
To play with things
And we almost missed the whole point!

Now, I can play with the sun, the stars, the rivers, the trees.
Oh, what wonder!
And all the little animals on earth
And all "His creatures!"

God bless me daily with humuor and laughter
To enjoy your gifts
As I count all your blessings.

Choose Life

Mary Kennedy, PBVM
Newfoundland, 1999.

(Written at the end of a Creation-centred
Retreat held at St. Catherine's Renewal Centre, NL.)

NANO NAGLE

Nano is our mentor
Our guide along our way.
She speaks with gentle passion
To each of us today.
Her lantern keeps on burning
In hearts remaining true
To living out her vision
Though we may seem but few.

Her spirit still is with us.
And just as she did dare
To let the Spirit guide her
In going anywhere . . .
We, too, are called to witness, to love—
our lantern beam—
While continuing her mission
And living out her dream.

Dear Nano, please be present
With all upon this earth
Who join us in our mission
To bring God's love to birth.

Your children still are calling
To us who follow you
To free them from oppression,
Indignity and fear, too.

Give us the hearts of pilgrims
To go wherever sent
On mission and in ministry
Alive and with intent
To bring good news to others
Who crying to be fed
May truly share God's justice.

And meanwhile being led
To feed and nurture others
Who are your children dear.
Alive, we bring your spirit
To all both far and near.

Paula Delahunty, PBVM
Newfoundland,
Presentation Day, 2003.

SURRENDER

She said "Yes"
—not knowing
yet trusting.

Where will this lead?
What will this mean?

Does it matter?

Lifetime of "yeses"
that awaken
new vision—
    choices—
    challenges—
Birthing hope.

Moving forward.
Open, alive
Going "one pace beyond."

mould us and fashion us

Paula Delahunty, PBVM
Newfoundland,
November 29, 2003.

Nano Nagle,
　　eternally modern woman,
　　　　living in the Now of
　　　　　　poverty and repression
　　　　　　　　and doing something
　　　　　　　　　　about it.

Following where the Spirit led,
　　growing into answers and
　　　　not considering it
　　　　　　all a waste.

Loving God
　　beyond concern for self
　　　　knowing His work
　　　　　　would be done.

Loving,
　　exhorting,
　　　　strengthening,
　　　　　　serving her Sisters.

Because that is what
　　community is,
　　　　and always will be
　　　　　　about.

Nano
worthy of the praise
of a historian
and the song
of a poet

Australia Presentation Sister
(source unknown).

In the face of fear;
she chose to be daring,
In the face of anxiety,
she chose to trust,
In the face of impossibility
she chose to begin.
To universal misery,
she proposed ministry to persons;
To ignorance, knowledge;
To disllusionment,
tenacity of purpose;
And to multiple vexations,
singleness of heart.
Faced with failure,
she held fast to hope;
Faced with death,
she believed in a living future;
A programme for the future
she gave in one word:

LOVE

By Raphael Consedine, PBVM
Victoria, Australia.

NANO NAGLE

A cloud on the homes of Ireland—
The gloom of the Penal years—
A people outlawed and trampled,
And mocked for their sighs and tears,
A crime to kneel at the altar,
A crime to teach in the school;
Each daughter and son of Erin
Must be branded a slave, a fool.

> And then like a star of knowledge
> From the beautiful skies above,
> Came one to dispel the shadows—
> One strong in the strength of love;
> Who turned from the sunkissed highway,
> From comfort and ease and wealth,
> To walk in the sordid laneways,
> And to touch God's word by stealth.

Tell ye the tale of her victory,
Of her struggle 'gainst tyrant laws,
Of the glowing hearts she enlisted
To help in the holy cause;
Tell of the dark cloud lifted—
The cloud of despair and shame;
Tell of a woman's bravery,
Hold in your hearts her name.

> The story of Nano Nagle
> Is the story of Love and Faith,
> That win in the hardest battle,
> That triumph o'er sin and death,
> May ours be the grace to follow
> On the wearisome ways she trod,
> And to see her someday in Heaven,
> A Saint 'mong the Saints of God.

By Brian O'Higgins (Source Unknown).

In December 2002, the *Sunday Irish Tribune* held a competition with the intent of searching for the greatest Irish person of all times.

The competition was open to men and women in all walks of life. The poll included people from the worlds of art, writing, freedom fighters, scientists, and sports.

By a wide margin, the top one hundred had Nano Nagle, foundress of the Presentation Sisters of the Blessed Virgin Mary heading the list and being declared the winner. In fact, she outstripped her nearest runner-up, Michael Collins, the great Irish freedom fighter, by twice the votes.

On Friday, June 24, 2005, in a similar poll, Nano Nagle was again voted the Greatest Irish Woman of All Time.

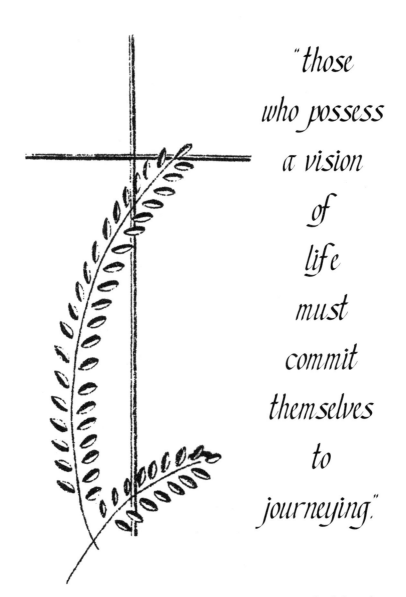

"those
who possess
a vision
of
life
must
commit
themselves
to
journeying."

Sr. Raphael Consedine
Australian Presentation.

WE ARE CALLED TO BE:

Women of the Lord . . .
Women who laugh and dance and
    sing . . .
Women who weep
    Not because we have lost
        something
    but because we have been
        given so much . . .
Women who struggle for justice . . .
Women faithful in prayer . . .
Women whom the spirit continues
    to disturb . . .
Women who are warm-hearted
    with the capacity to accept
    and forgive all who belong to
    the same imperfect and yet
    wondrous family . . .
Women who know what it means to
    give life for life . . .
Women striving to become . . .
Women who are a sign that the good
    news has come . . .
Women who dream dreams and continue
    to make promises . . .

Written by a Presentation Sister
(Source unknown).

"If I could be of any service in saving souls in any part of the globe, I would willingly do all in my power."

Nano Nagle

PRESENTATION GLOBAL PRESENCE

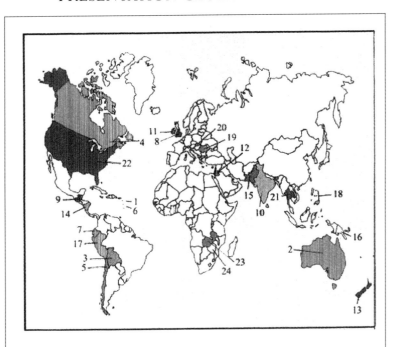

Key to Countries

1 - Antigua
2 - Australia
3 - Bolivia
4 - Canada
5 - Chile
6 - Commonwealth of Dominica
7 - Ecuador
8 - England

9 - Guatemala
10 - India
11 - Ireland
12 - Israel
13 - New Zealand
14 - Nicaragua
15 - Pakistan
16 - Papua New Guinea

17 - Peru
18 - Philippines
19 - Romania
20 - Slovakia
21 - Thailand
22 - United States
23 - Zambia
24 - Zimbabwe

Updated November 2005

IV

From Our Presentation Archives

Mission Statement

In response to the call of the Father
Rooted in Christ,
And empowered by the Holy Spirit,
We, Sisters of the Presentation,
Commit ourselves
To give radical expression
To the message of the Gospel.
Supported by life in community,
Strengthened by prayer,
And in collaboration with others,
We participate in the mission
    of the Church
Through our ministries of
    teaching,
    healing,
    and caring.
In imitation of Mary, our Patroness,
and in the spirit of Nano Nagle, our
Foundress,
We witness to Christ the Liberator
And bring a compassionate presence
to the poor and oppressed of our time.

Charism Statement

(Sisters of the Presentation)

The Call
Of the
Sisters of the Presentation
Is to be
Women of Contemplation
Living in Community
United in Charity
Joyfully and Generously
Serving
God's People
With
Special Attentiveness to the Poor

PRESENTATION SYMBOLS

The Coat of Arms of The Presentation Sisters

The Nagle Coat of Arms has the horizontal bar in azure blue design with three diamonds in gold. The oak design predominates. In heraldry, gold denotes generosity and elevation of mind, azure-blue signifies loyalty and truth, green signifies hope.

The Presentation Sisters adoped the Nagle Coat of Arms with some modifications. The goldfinch is supplanted by the Cross and effulgence as found on the ring worn by Presentation Sisters are symbols of faith and strength.

The two sprays of oak are symbolic of growth and the two skeins binding them together denote union. On the scroll is inscribed the Nagle Motto: *Non Vox sed Votum*—freely translated "Not Words, But Deeds."

The Ring

In 1855, Pope Pius IX granted permission to the Presentation Sisters to wear the ring. Regarding a motto for the ring, he said: "The Cross will supply for all."

When the ring was first given to the Sisters, it was presented with the words: "The Cross, by which your rings are distinguished from all others, denotes that crosses and contradictions are our portion in this life, but the effulgence around it reminds us that the Cross brings with it its own sweetness."

Presentation Sisters throughout the world can be recognized by this ring.

The Pin

Another symbol of Presentations Sisters today is a distinctive pin (also worn as a pendant).

This symbol is in the shape of a cross—another reminder of the significance of the Cross bringing fullness of life.

The letters (PBVM) on the pin conform to a circular pattern suggesting the continuity of commitment within the structure of our congregation and are intertwined to symbolize our unity in community. The letters are superimposed on a square, the square calling to mind that Christ is the cornerstone on which we are founded.

Each corner of the Cross (sign of our rootedness in Christ) forms the letter "M," reminding us of Mary, Mother of God, our Patroness, under whose protection we have placed ourselves and our congregation.

Pin of Presentation Associates

The Presentation Associate pin has a very special meaning behind its design. The centre of the pin is the same design as the Cross worn by the Sisters of the Presentation (PBVM).

Encircling that Cross, touching all four "arms," are the words "Presentation Associates."

The Cross of the Sisters was chosen for the centre because the Sisters are the core of the Association. The Sisters have extended their ministries to all four corners of the world, represented by the four "arms" of the Cross. The Presentation Associates are encircling the Sisters. Bonded together as Associates of the congregation they, by their prayer and good works, add support and strength to our ministry. At the same time they share in our prayer, friendship, and spiritual benefits.

This pin was designed by Dianne Geisen.

*I will go, Lord,
if you lead me . . .
I will
hold
your people*

in my heart!

Our Presentation spirituality recognizes that we have inherited Nano's love for the Sacred Heart of Jesus and that we are called to have hearts for justice and compassion. Let us pray for the courage of conversion. We have not seen Jesus, and yet we truly see Him every time we look at the broken bodies of our sisters and brothers. We have not heard Jesus, and yet we truly hear Him every time we hear the cries uttered by women and children and men in pain. We have not touched Jesus, and yet we truly touch Him every time we touch all those who come to us in loneliness.

In the midst of all human brochettes and human pain, we see, hear, and touch the heart of humanity, Jesus's humanity, the humanity of all persons embraced by His love. Adapted from Henri J. M. Nouwen, in *Heart Speaks to Heart* (Presentation Sisters, West Australia).

To be Presentation

is to be a

Prayerful

Presence

in the World

IMPORTANT FACTS ABOUT NANO NAGLE

Date of Birth .... April 9, 1718

Died .... April 26, 1784

Date of Baptism ...... April 10, 1718, at Monanimy Church

Baptism .... Honora (called Nano)

Place of Birth .... Ballygriffin on the River Blackwater,
near Mallow, Co. Cork.

Father .... Garret Nagle, Esquire descended from an
old Anglo-Norman family

Mother .... Ann Nagle (nee Matthews) of Thomastown,
near Thurles, Co. Tipperary

Relations ...• The Poet, Edmund Spencer (cousin) who lived
close to Nano's Home in the castle of Kilcolman
where he composed the "Faerie Queen."

• The Statesman and Politician, Edmund Burke
(cousin) under Sir Richard Nagle (grand-uncle),
Speaker of the Irish House of Commons, under

James II, Attorney General and an ardent Royalist (he was a leading figure in the Catholic Revival under James II).

• Pierce Nagle (grand uncle), High Sherriff of Cork.

• Father Theobald Matthew, Capuchin (cousin), Apostle of Temperance.

• Archbishop Chichester, S. J. (Rhodesia), great-great-grandnephew of Nano Nagle. He invited the Presentation Sisters to make a foundation in Rhodesia (1948).

Education ... In her home. (possibly a hedge school) and in France (possibly with the Ursulines) 1732 plus.

Final return from Paris .... 1747 – Nano had remained in the French capital for a number of years

Introduced the Ursulines into Ireland 1771

Founded the Presentation Congregation 1775

Tributes Down the Years to Nano Nagle

Excerpts form *Nano Nagle: A Story of Faith and Courage*
Sister Pius O'Farrell abd Sister Therese Halliden
Presentation Sisters, Ireland.

HUNDREDS OF ORPHANS

What will become of the innocent orphans, hundreds of whom she drew from vice and ignorance? What will become of the sick, naked and afflicted, whom she often relieved and comforted with her unbounded charities? The object of greatest distress was that of her greatest compassion.

Sr. Ursula Kavanagh, one of the first Irish Ursulines

A TENDER MOTHER

The doctors would not permit her to receive the Last Sacraments till about seven hours before she died, lest . . . her extraordinary devotion would exhaust her too much, as they still had hopes that God would spare her longer to the poor and distressed to whom she was a tender mother.

Sr. Angela Fitzsimons, the first Irish Ursuline

COMFORTING WORDS

We have the comfort to hear from the best divines in this city that there never was so much good done since St. Patrick's time as has been promoted by our holy Foundress' Establishments as they say it is the only counterpoise to the Charter Schools.

Sr. Angela Collins, successor to Nano Nagle

AFFLICTED WITH SORES

But it seems that every action of this great woman was to be productive of a hundredfold, for a plaster she applied to poor creatures afflicted with sores is still administered to them with most general spiritual advantage.

Sr. Clare Callaghan

NO STONE OR MONUMENT

Deeds of valour are perpetuated on canvas and heroism has become immortal in marble and the pen of genius has been employed to commemorate the achievements of many a field where thousands have fought and bled. But for the meek retiring benefactress of her race, whose career of usefulness has been among the hovels of the poor, whose path of duty led her along the dingy cottage floor or up the garret stair, that world of which she scarce was worthy has no stone or monumental bust and the eulogy of her virtues if written, must be only by Him who has promised that one cup of cold water, given in His name, shall not lose its reward.

Dean Dominic Murphy of Cork, 1845

THE DEBORAH OF IRELAND

This the mind of Nano Nagle grasped, this great mystery filled her intellect with thoughts, filled her heart with desires and with love and so she devoted herself and her fortune, her enlightened and trained intellect, her health, her strength, her life to this great work.

She is strictly and historically truly the mother of Irish Catholic education. She is the Deborah who turned the tide, the woman who took up the lance that had fallen from the hands of the brave and the strong . . .

Rev. Thomas Burke, OP, 1877

A PIONEER OF POPULAR EDUCATION

It is to the work of Nano Nagle who, though other organizations have taken up the task she began and other agencies have carried it out on a scale that even she did not foresee, nevertheless must still be given the glory of being the mother of popular education among the Catholic peoples who speak the English tongue.

Rev. P. C. Yorke, San Francisco, 1894

THE HEART OF JESUS

No doubt it was only in firm reliance on the Heart of Jesus that our young apostle could face the physical labour of her mission, to say nothing of its more repulsive features. . . . The great devotion to the Sacred Heart that prevails in the Presentation houses may be tracked back to the days of the Foundress. . . . This much we know for certain, that of fifty houses of the Presentation Order there is not one without its confraternity of the Sacred Heart. . . . Such are a few items in the life of her who, perhaps, did more than any other person to spread devotion to the Sacred Heart in Ireland.

Sr. Teresa Austin Carroll, RSM, 1867

BREAKING OF MORN

Gerald Griffin had sung. She heralded it. But must the shadow of an ungrateful forgetting keep forever hidden Nano Nagle, one of Ireland's greatest women?

Rev. H.A. Mc. Hugh, CSSR

VISION

The life of Nano Nagle presents two most remarkable features. The first is the vision which prompted this well-born, once wealthy woman to persevere for almost thirty years in the task of giving Catholic education to the children of the poor, at a time when such work still hovered on the verge of illegality and was regarded as risky by all but most courageous Catholics. . . . The second is the phenomenal expansion of the order which she founded. At her death in 1784 there was but one convent. . . .

Fr. Fergal McGrath, SJ

HIS GREATEST GRAND-AUNT

Nano was the aunt of Mary Honora French who became the wife of Charles J. Chichester. They were the grandparents of Bishop Aston Chichester of Rhodesia, now called Zimbabwe, so Nano was his great grand-aunt. He did much to help African woman to emerge from the custom of always being under tutelage.

PERFECT HARMONY

In the life of Nano Nagle there is perfect harmony between work and worship.

Fr. Henry Peel, OP

SOME SHAFTS OF LIGHT

While eighteenth-century Ireland did not offer optimum conditions for the practice of the religious life, some shafts of light broke the prevailing gloom. One was the appearance in Cork of two religious communities, the Ursuline and Presentation Sisters . . . founded by a true *mulier fortis*, Nano Nagle.

Fr. Hugh Fenning, OP

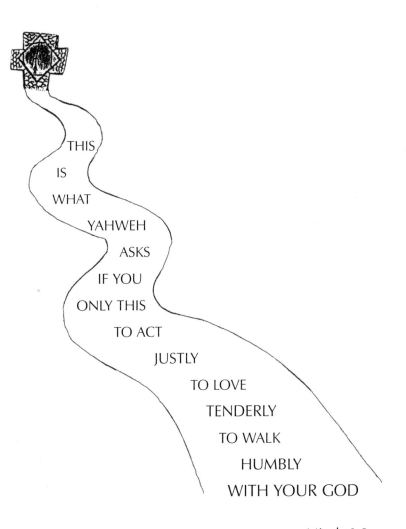

THIS
IS
WHAT
YAHWEH
ASKS
IF YOU
ONLY THIS
TO ACT
JUSTLY
TO LOVE
TENDERLY
TO WALK
HUMBLY
WITH YOUR GOD

Micah 6:8

SOME DAY
AFTER MASTERING
THE WINDS, THE WAVES,
THE TIDES, AND GRAVITY,
WE SHALL HARNESS FOR GOD
THE ENERGIES OF

LOVE

AND THEN
FOR THE SECOND TIME
IN THE HISTORY OF THE WORLD
WE WILL HAVE DISCOVERED

FIRE

Teilhard
(Source Unknown)

Quotations from Nano

1. If everyone thought as little of labour as I do, they would have little merit.

2. You see it has pleased the Almighty to make me succeed, when I had everything as I may say, to fight against.

3. If I could be of any service in saving souls in any part of the globe, I would willingly do all in my power.

4. The Almighty is All-sufficient.

5. The Almighty permits this to try your patience.

6. Providence has ordered everything for the best.

7. We must think the Almighty permits everything for the best.

8. I must say, every disappointment we have had, the Almighty has been pleased to make it turn out to our advantage; though my impatience very often made me not submit to His Divine will as I ought.

9. . . . with the assistance of God we may do a great deal.

10. It's all in the power of the Almighty; we don't know what is best for us and so we ought to be resigned to the Divine Will.

11. I think there is no greater happiness in the world than to be in union. Whoever we live with, we must expect to have something to suffer as this world is not to be our paradise.

12. The Almighty makes use of the weakest means to bring about His works.

13. I think none can tend more to His honor and glory in the world than it (our rule) does.

14. I hope we will show the world that nothing makes us go out only where charity obliges us.

15. I hope I shall have no reason to repent of the choice I have made as my first motive was charity.

16. We must leave it to the Almighty, He will do everything for the best in it . . .

17. It is a good sign of our future success that we should meet with crosses in the beginning.

18. I hope the Almighty will direct what is most to His honor and glory.

19. Divine providence does everything for the best . . .

20. The best works meet with the greatest crosses.

Nano's Scriptural References and Quotations That Have Formed Presentation Spirituality

The Scriptural references have been taken from the Rules of 1793 and 1947.

1. "Let the little children come to me; do not stop them; for it is to such as these that the kingdom of God belongs." Mark 10

2. ". . . whoever welcomes the one I send welcomes me . . ." John 13:20

3. ". . . love one another, just as I have loved you." John 13:34

4. ". . . be united in your convictions and united in your love, with a common purpose and a common mind . . ." Phil. 2:2

5. "Love is always patient and kind; it is never jealous; love is never boastful or conceited; it is never rude or selfish; it does not take offence, and is not resentful. Love takes no pleasure in other people's sins but delights in the truth; it is always ready to excuse, to trust, to hope and to endure whatever comes . . ." 1 Cor. 13: 4–7

6. "So stay awake, because you do not know the day when your master is coming . . ." Matt. 24:42

7. ". . . never say or do anything except in the name of the Lord Jesus . . ." Col. 3:17

8. "Whatever you eat, whatever you drink, whatever you do at all, do it for the glory of God." 1 Cor. 10:31

9. "I live now not with my own life but with the life of Christ who lives in me . . ." Gal. 2:19

10. "Come to me, all you who labor and are overburdened, and I will give you rest." Matt. 11:28

Nano Nagle, foundress of the Presentation Congregation, near the South Gate Bridge and Cork City Jail.

Nano crossed this bridge on her way to some of her schools. She remembered the inmates of the Jail in her will.

(Original by Con O'Sullivan is in St. Finbar's Parish Church, Cork.)

Grave of Nano Nagle at
South Presentation Convent, Cork, Ireland.

Mother M. de Sales talks of education in Newfoundland in 1882 to NTA President, Brother A. F. Brennan and Journal Editor, Harry Cuff.
(Picture compliments of Newfoundland Teachers' Association Journal.)

I feel this little book would not be complete without a few words about this great lady who was elected our Mother General for two terms of office (1931–1943). It was to her I applied for entrance in 1934. Born in Tralee, County Kerry, Ireland, she came to Newfoundland at the age of fifteen to join the Presentation Congregation. What a gracious, caring, prayerful lady she always was! Her long life was spent in teaching, especially music. In her later years, she always showed her interest in everything and had a special love for reading and music. She died in 1970 at the great age of 104.

The Veiled Virgin by Giovanni Strazza.

Displayed at Presentation Motherhouse, Cathedral Square, St. John's, NL, is a beautiful and rare piece of marble sculpture. It was done by the renowned, internationally famed sculptor Giovanni Strazza in Rome, Italy.

Strazza was born in Milan in 1818. He spent eighteen years working in Rome before returning to Milan where most of his works of art were done and where he died in 1875. It was during his years in Rome that this particular gem was done. It is signed in the marble at the back: Gio Strazza, Roma.

This sculptured marble statue, "The Veiled Virgin," was imported from Rome in 1856, by Most Rev. John Thomas Mullock, OSF, Bishop of St. John's, Newfoundland. An entry in Bishop Mullock's diary (in the Archdiocesan Archives), dated December 4, 1856, reads:

Received safely from Rome a beautiful statue of the Blessed Virgin Mary, in marble, by Strazza. The face is veiled, and the figure and features are all seen. It is a perfect gem of art.

This magnificent piece of art was given by Bishop Mullock in 1862, to the Superior of Presentation Convent, Cathedral Square, Mother M. Magdalen O'Shaughnessy—one of the four founding members, of the Congregation of the Sisters of the Presentation of the Blessed Virgin Mary, in Newfoundland (1833). The Bishop's sister, Sister M. de Pazzi, was a professed member of the community at the time.

The "Veiled Virgin" is kept in a large, highly protected glass case and is available for viewing all year long. It is written up in the tourist brochures, so during the summer season literally thousands of people come to see it. Don't miss an opportunity to view this treasure. It is actually impossible to describe the wonder of it. It indeed "has to be seen to be believed."

The following is an interesting account written by Sister Catherine Sullivan when she, Sister Marie Ryan, and Sister Dorothy Snow visited Ireland to represent Newfoundland Presentations at our bicentennial of Foundation in Cork, Ireland, 1976:

Dear Sisters:

During my two and a half weeks in Ireland and five days in Lourdes, I kept a record of events and impressions with the idea in mind that perhaps they might be of interest to those at home. I am sending these notes along, sketchy and unpolished as they are, with the hope that, should you have a spare moment to glance over them, you may be able to form some idea of what was for Sister Marie, for Sister Dorothy and for me a never-to-be forgotten experience.

We had a wait of five hours in Gander so there was a very pleasant stay with our Sisters and supper at the Convent before the flight at 10:00 p.m. The crossing, five and half hours, seemed brief as we were flying into the dawn which came at 2:30 a.m. by Newfoundland time. Heathrow is too big and too bewildering to talk about!

Our flight to Cork would not be until 6:00 p.m. so we found our way to St. George's Chapel at the airport. After consulting the schedule, we were disappointed to see that the Holy Thursday Liturgy would be at six, and of course we would miss it. We decided to take a tour of London but just missed one tour bus and could not wait for the next one. So back to the airport and to Aer Lingus for Ireland. We took a taxi to Douglas Street and, as the Sisters were at Holy Thursday Liturgy, we were admitted to South Presentation by a man who likes to lend a hand now and then about the place. We waited in the main parlour which used to be a dormitory of the Ursuline boarding school and where the relics and souvenirs of Mother Nagle are kept. The Sisters gave us a warm welcome—then supper and bed. The building where we slept is part of the original convent built by Nano Nagle for the Ursulines. Before the year of their arrival from France was over, the Ursulines had built, at right angles to the original structure, a boarding school for girls of wealthy families. "This" said one of the Sisters to us, "was Nano's darkest and bitterest hour, when she realized that the Ursulines were not prepared to do the work of her heart." However, God's plan was the establishment of a new congregation in the Church in Ireland and her disappointment was the stepping-stone to this foundation.

The convent is fascinating, with staircases, arches, passages, the "Blue Door," the "Green Door," "Nano Nagle's Door" etc. etc. There is a room called the "Nano Nagle Room," small and rather dingy, just inside what is now the back door but which must have been the main entrance of the Ursuline Convent. Mother Nagle would sit there and talk to the pupils.

The house nearer Douglas Street, and now known as Nano Nagle House, has an interesting history. It was built in 1810 after Nano's death and replaced the small convent she had built in 1777. There is still standing a wall surmounted by a Celtic Cross which building experts have assured the Sisters is part of that first little Institute of

Charitable Instruction. In 1825 the Ursulines secured some property in Blackrock (Nagle property by the way; that family was enormously wealthy!) and built a boarding school there. The Presentation Sisters then acquired the convent Nano had built for the Ursulines in 1771 and that is the building that is now known as South Presentation. The Sisters gave their own Convent on Cove Lane to the Presentation Brothers, a branch of Edmund Ignatius Rice's foundation. The brothers built a school for boys and a chapel, both attached to the original structure. It was because of those later additions that the Sisters, instead of simply getting back their own building, were obliged to buy the complex a few years ago when the brothers moved to Turner's Cross. The building, Nano Nagle House, is now being used as a hostel for Sisters of various congregations studying at Cork University.

You must not suppose that we neglected to visit the grave. Indeed, this was almost our first privilege. Over the stone slab there is a sliding glass panel which, when drawn aside, shows the coffin quite plainly. The children come in and drop notes ("Please, Mother Nagle, help me pass my exams please, please, please"!), and flowers down on the coffin. On Saturday while we were there with some American Sisters, a man came in to pray, accompanied by a "music man" almost like the travelling minstrels of long ago. He was evidently educated and cultured but was now homeless, and unkempt. However, he took out a flute and played with the most poignant sweetness, "Faith of our Fathers" and "Hail, Queen of Heaven," I have a picture of him.

In Cove Lane, now Douglas Street, there is a plaque, recently erected to the memory of Nano Nagle. A short distance down from Cove Lane is St. Finbarr's Church, the Parish Church of Nano when she lived in Cork. Her name is twice in the baptismal register as being sponsor for two children. The Church has been completely renovated, but it is essentially the same structure as it was more than two hundred years ago.

We crossed the River Lee over the bridge she must have taken when she visited her schools on the north side of the city and there we saw some very beautiful churches, among them St. Augustine's and the Franciscan Church of St. Francis. I must remember to say that the Sisters have all Holy Week services in their own chapel. The Easter Vigil was particularly impressive. All gathered outside the chapel in the passage which was in darkness except for a small fire burning in a sort of a brazier and a lighted flashlight held by one of the Sisters for the celebrant, a Capuchin from Holy Trinity, across the river. After the blessing, the candles were lit and we all proceeded to the chapel—very beautiful.

EASTER SUNDAY was a surprise. Just after breakfast, we three and Sister Rosina from California, but presently studying in Rome, were taken around the Ring of Kerry in the small bus the Sisters use to bring the deaf children to school from the house in Turner's Cross where they sleep. We had lunch in a homey little inn with a peat fire in the waiting room at a place in Bantry called Ballielickie. (My foot was on my native heath since Bantry is O'Sullivan territory).

County Kerry does not have the gentle contours and the rich green fields of Cork. It is rugged and poor agriculturally, but it does have the Lakes of Killarney. Also for miles the road is bordered with golden furze or gorse and, now and then, with banks of white hawthorn. We drove through six tunnels in solid rock, one of them rather long and scary. The weather was not good, and in fact there was a mild rain for part of the way, so not just right for pictures. At a place called "Moll's Gap" we found a souvenir shop open for business (although Easter Sunday) and I bought some prepared slides for our school library and a few of Nano Nagle stamps which we had been unable to get at the Post Office. There was Waterford glass there too which, of course, was out of the question, and magnificent wool "fleeces"—everything very costly. I think it was before we came to Moll's Gap that we stopped at a small cottage where Sister Margaret had to see the mother of a deaf boy. The Lakes of Killarney are beautiful but not any more so, I think, than our own in Newfoundland.

MONDAY, sunny, so we managed to get pictures of Nano Nagle's grave and various points of interest around the garden. At 11:30 a photographer came to take pictures of all the Sisters grouped, after which we were taken to the Convent at Turner's Cross for dinner and then to Ballygriffin. The Nagle property is extensive and rich looking but of the house where Nano was born, there is only a large grass-grown depression. There is a barn of sorts behind the place where the house stood, and there is a little stile over the stone wall around the estate. Nano must have climbed it many times when she was a "wild little girl." All through the countryside are numerous castles, many almost in ruins but others in fairly good condition. The only one we had a chance to examine closely, but not enter, was Monanimy, an old castle once occupied by Knights Templar. In 1358, the Nagles acquired the land around the castle, and the castle itself, from Lord Roche (we passed through the village of Castletownroche to reach Monanimy) and David Nagle had lived there, so, in much later years Nano must have visited. The castle, in fact, was still occupied in the 1930's until a fire destroyed the interior. It is owned now by an American from Oklahoma who lives in a house close by. There are danger signs posted and he has put barbed wire around the lower windows and the main door. Another castle we saw along the way was Carriganna Castle, very well preserved even to glass in the small narrow windows and with roof and chimneys intact. On the way back we had supper, a salad plate, at Central Inn, Mallow, and I do think I kept judging all the young men I saw coming and going by the familiar old song "Rakes of Mallow." There was a showing of the film "Nano" after we got back. I love it. The actors, Mother de Sales told us, stayed at the hostel on Douglas Street while they worked in Cork and all wept when they were leaving, Sister Anne had been so beautifully kind to them.

TUESDAY: APRIL 20. Our pictures are in the Cork Examiner but that, of course, the least important event of the day. In the morning we went down town to St. Patrick Street to the bank and to see the shops. At 3:00 p.m. in St. Finbarr's Church was the special Mass concelebrated by six bishops, the Bishop of Cork being principal celebrant. The Gloria, Sanctus and Agnus Dei were sung in Irish (I have discovered that the Sisters prefer to have their language called "Irish" rather than "Gaelic") It was very, very beautiful. What a sweet but forceful language it is! Sister Marie was farseeing enough to have brought a tape recorder and she has a tape of the choir as well as Father Walsh's splendid homily on the life and works of Nano Nagle. After Mass everyone went to the grave and we noticed and photographed one touching little scene. Among the dignitaries, the President of Ireland, the Mayor of Cork, bishops and other officials was one stooped, shabby little woman standing still and silent, gazing on the coffin. We all thought how appropriate her presence was since Mother Nagle had a particular love for poor and lonely old women and in fact established, the year before she died, an almshouse for them in Cove Lane. The Presentation Sisters cared for the old people there until 1887 when the Little Sisters of the Poor came to Cork to undertake this charitable work. The building, still called the Almshouse, was converted into a school.

Dinner in the school auditorium was quite a grand affair but the President's speech, being entirely in Irish, except for one sentence, an allusion to the American Bicentenary, was incomprehensible to me. Immediately after dinner we went down to the quays to the Cork Music School where a play was staged—the entire life of Nano Nagle very beautifully produced. We had pictures taken with the actress who played the lead in the film "Nano" and met Sisters from various parts of Ireland.

WEDNESDAY, went to a travel agency to arrange for our trip to Lourdes. There was to be a pilgrimage leaving Dublin for Lourdes so we decided to go to Galway on our way to Dublin. In the afternoon, Mass again at St. Finbarr's with a very inspiring sermon by a Dominican. Another dinner and the play again at night.

THURSDAY: Went to Blarney by bus. On the way a Mr. McCarthy became very interested in Nfld. and the reason for our being in Ireland. In Blarney he insisted on taking us to the hotel for refreshments after which he directed us to the castle and advised us where to take the bus back to Cork. The Sisters had told us there wasn't much to see and we might be disappointed, but of course they are accustomed to castles all over the countryside. Blarney Castle is utterly fascinating, very large and clearly marked with signs to tell what each part is: Family Room, Chapel, Kitchen and horror! Murder Room. Huge, rather crude steps cut in the stone, go winding up to the thickness of the wall and smaller flights lead abruptly to cave-like rooms here and there. Although I'm sure there is no danger, I found kissing the Blarney Stone a very alarming experience. When we came down, breathless and dizzy, we met a missionary Brother in the little shop near the castle. He had come to collect from his missionary box, one of several to be found in souvenir shops.

There were interesting sights and sounds around Cork, one, for example, a tower quite near the convent, part of the 14th century monastery called the Red Abbey. There is a brass plate commemorating a battle fought by troops whose leader watched its progress from the top of this tower. There are so many beautiful churches to visit plus the open market, the River Lee itself, and always the snatches of conversation overheard with the soft rise and fall of the Cork accent. There was enough to see and hear in the days before leaving for Galway, Dublin, and Lourdes but a very particular privilege, we thought, was to meet Father Walsh author of "Nano Nagle and the Presentation Sisters" and to be taken by him to his house in Blackrock and to the Ursuline Convent. Here we had tea after which we handled and read Nano Nagle's letters so jealously guarded by the Ursulines who regard her as their foundress in Ireland.

SUNDAY APRIL 25: By bus to Galway. It was beautiful to watch the fields and hedges so uniquely and incredibly green, the miles of golden furze and here and there, more often than in Cork, a thatched-roof cottage. We walked from the bus station in Galway to the Convent with two young Mercy Sisters as willing guides and were given the usual beautiful welcome by our Sisters. It is the same Convent from which the Sisters left for Nfld. in 1833 and we read in the Annals the too-brief account of their departure, and a single short paragraph a few pages further on referring to the fact that two other Sisters joined the Nfld. mission in 1843. I remind myself, however, that the Nagle motto was "Deeds, not Words."

MONDAY: Left Galway at 12:35 p.m. by train to Dublin and went to Nagle House on Calderwood Road. This is the administrative headquarters for the Sisters in India. Again that marvelous welcome we had come to expect! After supper, we walked up Griffith Avenue an immensely long, straight street, wide and open so unlike the narrow roads of Cork and found our way to All Hallows to visit the Nfld. seminarians but they had not yet returned from Easter vacation. Next day we visited our Sisters in George's Hill, a very depressed area of Dublin. Mother Brendan showed us their greatest treasure—a crucifix carried by St. Francis Xavier on his missionary journeys. We had lunch and dinner in the city, then back to Nagle House until time to go again to All Hallows. You must try to imagine the joy of the young men at seeing faces from home—a great deal of talk and laughter and excitement until, as it was getting late, we were really obliged to leave, and they had to go off to study and night prayer. First, however, they had us promise to come back next day for dinner so we changed plans a little. We had only to see the Mercy Sisters in Baggott Street and our flight to Lourdes would not be until 10:00 p.m.

WEDNESDAY: We had naively supposed we were to have dinner at the seminary. Not so! Four of them (the other three, being third year students, had exams), took us to the Shelbourne Hotel where we had a very delicious dinner and for them as well as for us, a most enjoyable afternoon. They were very, very, good to us and so glad to see anyone from home where the heart always is! We went to St. Stephen's Green and to Gill's where they like to buy books or just browse—so we missed Baggott Street.

Wednesday night a late arrival in Lourdes and the next morning a very bad first impression with the shops and shops and more shops! However, at the shrine itself one can forget, being caught up and swept along in the tremendous tide of faith and love. I can't attempt to describe the Blessing of the Sick and the Torchlight Procession. These events have to be experienced in order to feel the full impact of Lourdes—devotion to the Most Blessed Sacrament through devotion to the Mother of God. One can never forget, too, the sight of so many afflicted people—a tiny blind child in our group and a wee little baby doomed to die in a few months of a rare and incurable liver ailment—the mothers so courageous and resigned! During the day, a walking tour of Lourdes to see Le Cachot, the house in which St. Bernadette was born and the mill where her father worked. There was grim poverty, such as we have never seen, or could even imagine. Unfortunately the kitchen of the home has been turned into a shop. Le Cachot, however, the miserable, abandoned prison where the family lived when the father was out of work, is untouched and there are preserved the few relics, the little cloak and stockings she wore and the small rosary she used.

FRIDAY: An excursion into Spain. I didn't feel like going so went to the Crypt in the morning and managed to find a small kneeling space near a pillar. There is Exposition of the Blessed Sacrament all day and the chapel is always thronged, even the aisles, with pilgrims in the most profound and reverent adoration. On my way back to the hotel, I bought the last of the slides for our school library. An Irish girl working in one of the shops helped me select them and then she gave me a small present. We've had a little fun over the fact that people in the street usually approach me for ten pence or a franc and I was taken by surprise to be receiving a gift. Mass at 11:00 a.m. in the Poor Clares Monastery Chapel directly across the street from the hotel. Father Lavallée asked me to read and we all sang familiar hymns. I went to the Blessing of the Sick at 4:30 p.m. and to the Torchlight Procession at 9:00. I had been asked by a priest who came around to the tables in the dining-room, to help with the English singing and, as we stood on the steps of the Holy Rosary Basilica, I had a magnificent view of the Rosary Square with its currents and cross-currents of light from the candles as the pilgrims moved back and forth. 10,000 people in one pilgrimage had left the night before so the procession was not as long as the one of the preceding evening. Just about ten o'clock, the Sisters came back from Spain full of enthusiasm. It had been a very enjoyable and worthwhile trip.

SATURDAY: To the Crypt, then Mass at the Poor Clare's at 9:30 after which the way of the Cross at 10:00 led by Father Lavallée. This experience again passes description. The figures are larger-than-life, bronze, from eight to fourteen figures in each group—very, very beautiful. The way goes up and up, rocky and difficult as is fitting, to the 12th Station. One of the women carried in her arms a child who seemed to be autistic, and I shall never forget the mingling of grief, resignation and peace in the mother's face. There is a sharp descent to the 13th and 14th Stations, the latter being grouped in a very appropriate cave. It is no trouble to find caves about and in fact, after the stations, we went up a flight of steps and into a series of caves with altars and flowers. I can't think that any devotions can be held there, as there is constant dripping of water.

In the afternoon a bus tour to Governie, the last village on the border between France and Spain. The road follows the River Gave all the way and is very scenic, climbing steadily into the Pyrenees. The river itself becomes the merest stream but there are deep ravines, countless water-falls and meadows, not so green as Ireland's gorge, full of tiny wild daffodils. Half way to Governie there is a deep gorge spanned by a bridge which Napoleon III had built in 1860. At Governie is a perfumery where Chanel V is made and also a little medieval church dedicated to Our Lady of the Snows, quite appropriate in the shadow of the towering , snowcapped mountains. A small side chapel has a very old statue of Our Lady dating back the 14th century and titled "Notre Dame du Port." In a cabinet at the back of the chapel are skulls of Knights Templar. I met two ladies from New York in the graveyard outside and one of them told me she used to know two girls from Placentia—O'Reilly's. On the way back we sang songs—mostly Irish, but Sister Dorothy taught everyone "Jack Was Every Inch a Sailor." I went to the balcony after dinner to try for a good photo-graph of the Torchlight Procession but I'm afraid, not much success.

SUNDAY: Sister Marie and Sister Dorothy made a day of retreat and fasting. At nine there was Mass for all the nations, in the underground Basilica of Pius X which has a capacity of 20,000. We had been advised to go early so as to get a seat, but although I left the hotel shortly after eight there was not a place to be seen and people were already filling the aisles, the balconies and the steps. I managed to find a small corner of a kneeler. The Mass was sung in Latin—Mass VIII, very familiar to all. After lunch I went to the Crypt for a while, then to the Chapel of Reconciliation for Confession but there being no priest at the "English" confessionals, I did the way of the Cross again. There were two groups of pilgrims and several individuals making the stations, a man and a woman, I noticed, walking barefoot.

MONDAY: To the Crypt and to the Basilica of the Holy Rosary which is beneath it. The fifteen mysteries are in magnificent mosaics all around, each with its own altar. Near the front entrance I found a dark little passage leading to a small chapel dedicated to Our Lady of Perpetual Help. There were rather unusual pictures of saints adorning the walls. Sister Marie had already visited the parish church of Lourdes, so Sister Dorothy and I climbed the hill to see it. There is a sign on the front to say that St. Bernadette was baptized there, and a very much enlarged copy of the baptismal entry from the register.

Our door keys had to be handed in by noon so, until midnight, we were more or less "sans pays." I went for my last visit to the grotto and for once there was not a devotion of some kind in progress, so I could go inside the railing, kneel on the flagstones and say a rosary. The grotto is free from commercialism as only candles are sold. The statue is a little weathered and the rock, around which pilgrims walk in a slow and constant procession, is worn smooth by generations of reverent lips. In Lourdes it did not seem to be yet the time of roses but a bush growing from the rock near the statue had a single beautiful rose and under Our Lady's feet were some humble little purple flowers along with the dull pink pimpernel we used to call wild geranium. The last Mass for our group was to be at the City of the Poor, a short bus ride from Lourdes. A young Englishman, a volunteer as are all the workers there, showed us around. It is very beautiful, peaceful, clean and comfortable and completely free to pilgrims of all nations and all religions who cannot afford a hotel.

At 5:30 we had Mass in the chapel, a rough stone building with thatched roof. Benches inside were covered with sheepskins from sheep on the farm. During mass, Father Lavellée administered the Sacrament of the Sick to those needing medical care, about twelve adults and our pet, three-and-a-half-year-old Tracy, a bright, sunny, laughing little girl afflicted with leukemia. Back to the hotel for dinner at 7:00 p.m. then to the Rosary Square for the last Torchlight Procession, after which singing in the hotel foyer before taking the bus to the airport in Tarbes at midnight. Arrived in Dublin at 2:30 A.M. and a dreary wait until 8:30 when we took the train to Cork.

On Tuesday, Mother de Sales took us to Crosshaven to see Sister Carmel who spent some time last summer in Paris researching information on Nano Nagle. Her findings will be published eventually and will, I am sure, be extremely interesting.

THURSDAY: The last prayers at Mother Nagle's grave, the last good-bye to the dear Sisters at South Presentation, and faces turned towards home! No matter how interesting, how absorbing or fascinating an experience may be there comes a time when the call of home rings loud and persistent. Our homecoming was very beautiful with about twenty Sisters meeting us in Torbay, all the others at the front entrance of Cathedral Square, a banner of welcome on the wall and a very special cake!

This account is perhaps too long, and yet I know that there are a thousand vignettes overlooked, a million lights and shadows missing from the picture. I can only assure you that we remembered you always and prayed for you and for every wish of your heart. Sister Marie had to go off immediately on one of her retreat missions, Sister Dorothy went west to show the film "Nano," so I have undertaken the task of transcribing these notes. Thank you for your patience—if you've come to the end—and God bless you all.

Sister Catherine

(Sullivan, PBVM)

ACKNOWLEDGEMENTS

To our congregational leader, Sister Betty Rae Lee, and her council, my sincere thanks and deep appreciation for all their encouragement.

Sincere and grateful thanks to our archivist Sister Perpetua Kennedy, Ph.D., and her generous assistant, Sister Patricia Whittle, MA, for their help in research.

Very special and deep thanks also to Eileen Greenham, a dear friend of long standing. Without Eileen's gentle "pushing," this completed work would have appeared much later. She was the "wind beneath my wings." What an indefatigable worker! Your thoroughness, care, and insight were major factors bringing success to the early typing of this work. God bless you, Eileen.

To Sharon Blandford, Marcey Kane, and Barbara Barron, I owe a debt of gratitude. When in late autumn 2004 I had not resurfaced the idea of putting this work into print, you questioned my not pursuing my dream. Thank you for your inspiration, friendship, and gentle urging. May God bless you for all your kindness.

To my loved nephew, Frank Wyse, a generous computer specialist, I owe gratitude all along the way, as well as for taking the preprinting of this work into his capable hands. Special thanks to both Frank and his lovely wife, Christine Morrissey, for many hours of typing, formatting, and editing.

Nor can I forget the many weekend hours of meticulous proofreading generously done by a good friend, Gloria Harding, P.C.J., and a cousin Sister Lois Greene, PBVM. For their clear thinking, deep insight, and generous gift of time I am deeply grateful.

My thanks also to Chris Kane who generously and willingly came to my aid when I needed some extra computer help. Your spirit of generosity and thoughtfulness will carry you far.

For her interest, advice, and careful final work with this book, my sincere thanks to Marilyn Puddicombe. You came along as a lifesaver in the final stages of prepublication.

To Presentation Sisters of the Union, Monasterevan, County Kildare, Ireland, my sincere thanks for their ready and generous use of material, and especially Canon T. J. Walsh's outstanding book *Nano Nagle and the Presentation Sisters*, which they had republished in 1980. To Sister Immaculata Carr, PBVM, at North Presentation Convent, Cork, Ireland, for use of pictures from her delightful children's book *Nano Nagle: Lover of Children, Friend of the Poor*, my deepest appreciation. Both Sister Pius Farrell, PBVM, and Sister Therese Halliden, PBVM, gave me great help through use of their very encompassing work *Nano Nagle: A Story of Faith and Courage*. My sincere thanks. Sister Rosaria O'Callaghan, PBVM, of Aberdeen, South Dakota, whose community has been generous with permission to use material and photos from her excellent book *Flame of Love*, my deepest thanks. To the Presentation Sisters in Victoria, Melbourne, Australia, also, I am deeply grateful for permission to use poems by the late Sr. M. Raphael Consedine, PBVM, of loving memory, chiefly from her inspiring book *The Life of Nano Nagle: One Pace Beyond*

Special thanks to the staff of Flanker Press, especially Jerry Cranford, Dwayne LaFitte, Garry Cranford, and his lovely wife, Margo. Your patience, care, and interest are deeply appreciated.

Finally, to all those who helped in many and various ways, my deep appreciation and gratitude.

NOTES

1. Thomas J. Walsh, *Nano Nagle and the Presentation Sisters* (Monasterevan, Ireland: Presentation Generalate, 1996), 386.

2. Thomas J. Walsh, "Letter to Miss Fitzsimmons, 17 July 1769," in *Nano Nagle and the Presentation Sisters* (Monasterevan, Ireland: Presentation Generalate, 1996), 346.

3. Walsh, *Nano Nagle*, 50.

4. Sister M. Claude, "Historical Setting of the Presentation Order" (paper presented at a seminar in Drogheda, Ireland, 22 July 1972, mimeographed).

5. Ibid.

6. Ibid.

7. Ibid.

8. Ibid.

9. Ibid.

10. Ibid.

11. Thomas J. Walsh, reprinting Coppinger, "The Life of Miss Nano Nagle, 1794," in *Nano Nagle and the Presentation Sisters* (Monasterevan, Ireland: Presentation Generalate, 1996), 386.

12. Claude, "Historical Setting."

13. Ibid.

14. Sister Mary Pius, "Nano Nagle: Her Courage and Equanimity" (paper presented at a seminar in Drogheda, Ireland, 22 July 1972, mimeographed).

15. Walsh, reprinting Coppinger, 387.

16. Walsh, *Nano Nagle*, 91.

17. Ibid., 87.

18. Ibid., 88.

19. Ibid., 99.

20. Walsh, reprinting Coppinger, 389–90.

21. Walsh, *Nano Nagle*, 125.

22. Thomas J. Walsh, "Letter to Miss Mulally, 29 July 1780," in *Nano Nagle and the Presentation Sisters* (Monasterevan, Ireland: Presentation Generalate, 1996), 363–4.

23. Walsh, reprinting Coppinger, 391.

24. Walsh, *Nano Nagle*, 9.

25. Margaret Mary, PBVM, "Apostolate of the Presentation Sisters" (paper presented at a seminar in Drogheda, Ireland, 22 July 1972, mimeographed).

26. Thomas J. Walsh, "Letter to Miss Fitzsimmons from Bath, 20 July 1770," in *Nano Nagle and the Presentation Sisters* (Monasterevan, Ireland: Presentation Generalate, 1996), 353.

27. Walsh, *Nano Nagle*, 86.

28. Walsh, *Nano Nagle*, 96.

29. Walsh, *Nano Nagle*, 100.

30. Walsh, "Letter to Miss Mulally, 29 July 1780," 364.

31. Ibid.

32. Thomas J. Walsh, "Letter to Miss Mulally, 24 August 1778," in *Nano Nagle and the Presentation Sisters* (Monasterevan, Ireland: Presentation Generalate, 1996), 359.

33. Ibid.

34. Walsh, *Nano Nagle*, 52–3.

35. Ibid.

36. Ibid., 125.

37. Ibid., 119.

38. Walsh, "Letter to Miss Fitzsimmons, 17 July 1769," 346.

39. Thomas J. Walsh, "Letter to Miss Fitzsimmons, 17 December 1770," in *Nano Nagle and the Presentation Sisters* (Monasterevan, Ireland: Presentation Generalate, 1996), 355.

40. Ibid.

41. Thomas J. Walsh, "Letter to Miss Mulally, 29 September 1776," in *Nano Nagle and the Presentation Sisters* (Monasterevan, Ireland: Presentation Generalate, 1996), 357.

42. Ibid., 358.

43. Austin Flannery, ed., *Vatican Council II: The Conciliar and Post Conciliar Documents* (Northport, New York: Costello Publishing, 1975), 780.

44. Thomas J. Walsh, "Letter to Miss Fitzsimmons, early in 1770," in *Nano Nagle and the Presentation Sisters* (Monasterevan, Ireland: Presentation Generalate, 1996), 347.

45. Ibid.

46. Ibid., 348.

47. Thomas J. Walsh, "Letter to Miss Fitzsimmon, May 1770," in *Nano Nagle and the Presentation Sisters* (Monasterevan, Ireland: Presentation Generalate, 1996), 352.

48. Thomas J. Walsh, "Letter to Miss Fitzsimmons, 28 September 1770," in *Nano Nagle and the Presentation Sisters* (Monasterevan, Ireland: Presentation Generalate, 1996), 356.

49. Claude, "Historical Setting."

50. Walsh, "Letter to Miss Mulally, 29 September 1776," 358.

51. Ibid.

52. Walsh, *Nano Nagle*, 117.

53. Walsh, "Letter to Miss Fitzsimmons, 17 December 1770," 356.

54. Walsh, reprinting Coppinger, 393.

55. Walsh, *Nano Nagle*, 117.

56. Ibid., 118, footnote.

57. Ibid., 119.

58. Ibid., 127.

59. Gal. 4:19 (translation used in the Jerusalem Bible).

60. Walsh, *Nano Nagle*, 128–9.

61. *Christian Education of Youth: Encyclical Letter of Pius XI, 31 December 1929* (New York: Paulist Press, n.d.), 38.

62. Thomas J. Walsh, "Letter of Angela Collins to Miss Mulally," in *Nano Nagle and the Presentation Sisters* (Monasterevan, Ireland: Presentation Generalate, 1996), 370–71.

63. Corona Wyse, PBVM, "Nano Nagle: Ireland's Pioneer Teacher of Penal Days and Foundress of the Presentation Sisters" (paper written for Education 381, University of Ottawa, Ottawa, Ontario, Canada, 20 June 1959, mimeographed), quoting APN in *Lantern Beams*, 67.

64. Ibid.

65. Mary, "Apostolate."

66. Wyse, "Nano Nagle," quoting *Lantern Beams*, 72.

67. Ibid.

68. Walsh, *Nano Nagle*, frontispiece, quoting Jerome Kiely.

69. Edwina (Angela) Curtis, PBVM, "Ireland's Pioneer Educator and Social Worker: Nano Nagle" (essay presented to the Department of Education, St. Francis Xavier University,

Antigonish, Nova Scotia, Canada, 1 April 1968, mimeographed), quoting Gerald Griffin.

70. Mary James Dinn, PBVM, *Foundation of the Presentation Congregation of Newfoundland* (St. John's, Newfoundland: Merner Printing, 1975) 13, 15–20, 25–6.

71. Ibid., quoting *The Newfoundlander* no. 323 (26 September 1833).

72. Ibid., quoting from Sister Magdalen O'Shaunessy, St. John's, Newfoundland, 22 September 1833.

73. Ibid., quoting Most Rev. M. F. Howley, *Ecclesiastical History of Newfoundland* (Boston: Doyle and Whittle, 1888), 426.

74. Ibid., quoting *The Patriot*, St. John's, Newfoundland, October 1833.

75. Ibid., quoting *The Centenary of the Basilica of St. John the Baptist* (St. John's, Newfoundland: Robinson & Co., 1955), 225.

76. Ibid., quoting Dr. Frederick W. Rowe, *The Development of Education in Newfoundland* (Toronto: Ryerson Press, 1964), ix–225.

77. Ibid., quoting *Journal of the House of Assembly of Newfoundland* (St. John's, Newfoundland: n.p., 1863), 348.

78. Ibid., quoting *Journal of the House of Assembly of Newfoundland* (St. John's, Newfoundland: n.p., 1863), 349.

79. Ibid., citing Rowe, *Education in Newfoundland*, 119.

80. Ibid., citing Rowe, *Education in Newfoundland*, 126.

81. Dinn, *Presentation Congregation,* 26–7.

82. Wyse, "Nano Nagle."

83. Ibid.

84. First letters written by Sister Magdalene O'Shaunessy and Sister Xaverius Lynch from St. John's to Galway, Presentation Archives, St. John's, Newfoundland.

BIBLIOGRAPHY

APN, *Lantern Beams*. Bailieborough, Ireland: Presentation Sisters, 1956.

Browne, Rev. P. W., Ph.D. "Nano Nagle's Daughters." *Ave Maria* 38, no. 15 (1957).

Burke, Thomas, OP. Sermon delivered on the occasion of the Centenary of the Founding of the Presentation Congregation, 1875. Mimeographed.

Byrne, Sister Mary Matthew. *Pen-Pictures of Nano Nagle*. St. John's, Newfoundland: Robinson–Blackmore, 1975.

Carr, Immaculata, PBVM. *Nano Nagle, Lover of Children: Friend of the Poor*. Dublin, Ireland: Falens and Co., 1982.

Christian Education of Youth: Encyclical Letter of Pope Pius XI, 31 December 1929. New York: Paulist Press, n.d., 38.

Claude, M., PBVM. "Historical Setting up of the Presentation Order." Paper presented at a seminar in Drogheda, Ireland, 22 July 1972. Mimeographed.

Consedine, M. Raphael, PBVM. *One Pace Beyond: The Life of Nano Nagle*. Australia: Dove Communications Pty., 1977.

———. *Listening Journey*. Australia: Congregation of the Presentation of the Blessed Virgin Mary, 1983.

Curtis, Edwina (Angela), PBVM. "Ireland's Pioneer Educator and Social Worker: Nano Nagle." Essay presented to the Department of Education, St. Francis Xavier

University, Antigonish, Nova Scotia, Canada, 1 April
1968. Mimeographed.

Dinn, Mary James, PBVM. *Foundation of the Presentation
Congregation in Newfoundland.* St. John's, Newfoundland:
Merner Printing, 1975.

Flannery, Austin, ed. *Vatican Council II: The Conciliar and Post
Conciliar Documents.* Northport, New York: Castello
Publishing, 1975.

Galvin, Sister Mary Camillus. *From Acorn to Oak: A Study of
Presentation Foundations 1775-1968.* Fargo, North
Dakota: n.p., 1969.

Kiernan, Mary, PBVM. "Nano Nagle—Her Spirit." Paper
presented at a seminar in Drogheda, Ireland, 22 July
1972. Mimeographed.

Leahy, Maurice. *The Flower of Her Kindred: A Study of Nano Nagle
of Ireland.* New York: Etheridge Co., 1944.

Life of Nano Nagle. Dublin, Ireland: Irish Messenger Office, 1965.

Mary, Margaret, PBVM. "Apostolate of the Presentation
Sisters." Paper presented at a seminar in Drogheda,
Ireland, 22 July 1972. Mimeographed.

Murphy, Rev. Dominic. *Memoirs of Miss Nano Nagle and of the
Ursuline and Presentation Orders in Ireland.* Cork: Joseph
Roche, 1845.

O'Callaghan, Mary Rosaria, PBVM. *Flame of Love: A Biography
of Nano Nagle—Foundress of the Presentation Order
(1718-1784).* Milwaukee, Wisconsin: Bruce Press, 1960.

O'Farrell, Pius, PBVM, and Therese Halliden, PBVM. *Nano
Nagle: A Story of Faith and Courage.* Strasbourg, France:
Sadifa Editions, 1983.

O'Farrell, Sister Mary Pius. *Nano Nagle: Woman of the Gospel.* Monasterevin, Ireland: Presentation Generalate, 1996.

Pius, Mary, PBVM. "Nano Nagle: Her Courage and Equanimity." Paper presented at a seminar in Drogheda, Ireland, 22 July 1972. Mimeographed.

Walsh, Thomas J. *Nano Nagle and the Presentation Sisters.* Monasterevin, Ireland: Presentation Generalate, 1996.

Wyse, Corona, PBVM. "Nano Nagle: Ireland's Pioneer Teacher of Penal Days and Foundress of the Presentation Sisters." Paper written for Education 381, University of Ottawa, Ottawa, Ontario, Canada, 20 June 1959. Mimeographed.

ABOUT THE AUTHOR

Sister Corona Wyse was born in 1917 in Placentia, Newfoundland, and now resides at the convent in Gander. Having been educated by the Presentation Sisters through elementary and high school, in 1934 she heard the call to join them and serve God in the teaching profession. She taught in Grand Falls–Windsor and Corner Brook, and she served as director of religious education with the St. John's and Stephenville Roman Catholic School Boards. Her teaching also took her to the United States to the Graduate School of Education in the Catholic University of America, Washington, DC. She then worked as director of education with St. Pius Parish, Bowie, MD. In Roseau, Commonwealth of Dominica, West Indies, she taught at the Convent School and she held retreats and workshops at the Family Life Centre. Professionally, she holds masters degrees in educational administration, spiritual guidance, counselling, and pastoral studies. She also holds a doctorate in philosophy of education.